BEGINNER GARDENING
STEP BY STEP

DK

Editors Emma Tennant, Jane Simmonds
US Editor Megan Douglass
Project Art Editors
Mandy Earey, Charlotte Johnson
Managing Editor Dawn Henderson
Managing Art Editor Marianne Markham
DK Picture Library Emily Reid
Jacket Creative Steven Marsden
Producer Rebecca Fallowfield
Creative Technical Support
Sonia Charbonnier
Art Director Maxine Pedliham
Publishing Director Mary-Clare Jerram

First American Edition, 2019
Published in the United States by DK
Publishing
345 Hudson Street, New York, New York
10014

Copyright © 2018 Dorling Kindersley Limited
DK, a Division of Penguin Random House LLC
19 20 21 22 23 10 9 8 7 6 5 4 3 2 1
001–309889–Mar/2019

A catalog record for this book
is available from the Library of Congress.
ISBN 978-1-4654-7700-2

Printed and bound in China

A world of ideas:
see all there is to know
www.dk.com

CONTENTS

INTRODUCTION

Planting up your own patch of earth is a wonderful experience, but deciding what to grow in the land that lies before you can be a daunting task. For those starting out, filled with excitement at the idea of growing fruits and vegetables, or planting trees and flowers, this book provides the answers.

"Getting Started" will help you to get to know your space and choose plants that will grow well in particular soil types and conditions year after year. In "Flowers & Foliage" you'll learn the secrets of sowing seeds, be amazed by the versatility of container gardening, and discover how to make a new border. In "Lawns" you'll find out how to make the most out of possibly the largest part of the yard, while in "Grasses" you'll learn to nurture a distinctive group of plants.

As your confidence grows alongside your gardening knowledge and skills, you'll be encouraged to try more ambitious projects such as making a tower of flowers in "Climbers," shaping a topiary cone in "Shrubs," or planting and caring for your first tree in "Small Trees."

For many beginners, the idea of having your own patch of land will go hand in hand with growing your own fruits and vegetables. In these chapters, you'll take simple steps toward producing your first crops, with ideas designed for gardens of any shape or size. Herbs will quickly earn a place in your edible garden, whether in beds and borders, or in hanging baskets and window boxes.

The final chapter on "Practicalities" shows you how to water and feed your plants, and explains essential maintenance jobs to keep everything healthy and tidy and to protect your plants against pests and diseases.

Creating a yard that you can enjoy and keep looking good all year round is easier than you think! By following the steps and projects outlined in this book you will reap instant rewards and long-term successes so that you can enjoy your yard in all seasons.

GETTING
STARTED

WHICH WAY DOES
YOUR GARDEN FACE?

The direction in which your garden faces affects the amount of sun and shade it receives. Consider this when choosing your plants to ensure they will thrive in the conditions you have to offer.

KEY POINTS

- Trees, hedges, and shrub borders act as buffers. They slow the wind and provide shelter for plants and for people.

- A sunny spot can be enhanced with a raised bed to improve drainage for tender plants.

- A windy area can be sheltered with a permeable barrier, such as a trellis.

SEE ALSO

- **KNOW YOUR SOIL** >> 12/13
- **CHOOSE HEALTHY PLANTS** >> 20/21

EAST AND WEST

East-facing gardens are sunny but cold in the morning; hardy plants that like shade are a good choice here. West-facing walls and fences have sun in the afternoon and evening and offer milder growing conditions.

Simple observation of how much sun your garden receives will give an idea of its orientation. South-facing gardens receive the most sun, and north-facing sites the least. To determine it accurately, use a compass. Stand with your back to your house wall—the reading from here shows the direction your garden faces.

The amount of direct sun and the sun's position in the garden change as the day progresses. A south-facing garden will have sun all day, a north-facing one much less, perhaps none in winter. Sunny gardens are often more desirable, but shade does have its advantages. There are many wonderful shade-loving plants that prefer to be out of direct sun, such as *Mahonia* or cyclamen, while in a sunny garden, slightly tender plants from Mediterranean regions, for example, will flourish. The key is to work with what you have.

Morning: areas that are in sun now may be in shade by the afternoon.

Midday: the sun is overhead, so the yard receives maximum sun.

Evening: as the sun sets, the glancing light casts soft shadows.

KNOW **YOUR SOIL**

Understanding what kind of soil you have will help you to decide which plants will thrive in your garden and ensure the best results. You can always make improvements to your soil, but you also need to work with its basic type.

KEY POINTS

- **Finding out your soil's properties** saves time and money, enabling you to buy suitable plants.

- **Look around local gardens** and make a note of the plants that grow well in your area. These are all likely to be suited to your soil type and therefore an excellent indication of what will flourish in your own garden.

SEE ALSO

- **IMPROVE YOUR SOIL** >> 16/17
- **MAKE COMPOST** >> 234/235

THE PERFECT SOIL

All plants have different needs. However, loam—a mix of clay and sand—is generally seen as a good thing. Ideal soils also have a fairly neutral pH and contain a good amount of organic matter.

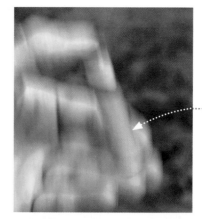

Testing acidic soil Acidic soils are lime-free, unlike limy, or slightly chalky, alkaline soils. Some plants will grow well in acidic soils, but others won't. Buy a soil pH test kit from a garden center to assess soil acidity. At home, take soil samples from around the garden. Shake each soil sample in the chemical solution, then leave the mixture to settle.

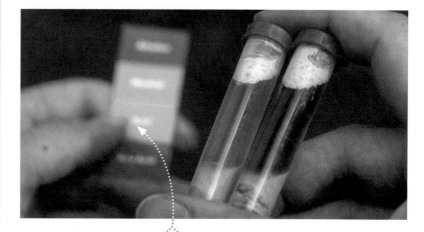

Determining acidity Match the color to the card in the test kit. The pH scale runs from 14 (very alkaline) to 1 (very acidic), with 7 being neutral.

Testing sandy soil Easy to turn and weed, sandy soils often heat up earlier in spring than clay soils. Their free-draining nature can be an asset for growing certain plants, but during heavy rainfall precious nutrients can be washed away. As a result, sandy soils may be quite low in nutrients. The more sand a soil contains, the more it will crumble when a handful is compressed, because it has very little of the sticky bonding agent supplied by clay particles. Soils with a high sand content will feel coarse, gritty, and dry when worked through your fingertips.

Test for sandy soil by rubbing earth through your fingertips. It will feel gritty.

Squeeze and release soil then press lightly with your thumb. Sandy soils will crumble.

Testing clay soil While clay soils are potentially the most fertile and productive, clay particles are extremely fine and slippery when wet, forming a dense paste that sticks to boots and garden tools. Soils that have a very high clay content can become waterlogged and "puddle" in wet weather, or set like concrete and crack in droughts. In such situations, clay soil can be greatly improved by adding plenty of grit and organic matter.

If you can mold your soil sample in your hands and get it to hold its shape, you have clay. When moistened, it feels slimy.

Rolling a sample into a sausage and bending it into a ring reveals a very clay soil.

Growing your own plants from seed is a simple and inexpensive way to fill your garden. First find out about your garden's aspect and soil, and then start to plan what you want to plant and grow.

IMPROVING
YOUR SOIL

Most garden soils benefit from some preparation before planting, as well as ongoing treatments to keep them fertile. Both heavy clays and light, sandy soils can be improved to help grow healthier plants.

KEY POINTS

- **Try not to walk on clay** when it is wet and sticky—you can damage the soil structure and worsen the drainage problem.
- **There's no use digging** rock-hard clay soil in summer, as the clods break up into dust.
- **Both very light** and very heavy soils benefit from annual additions of organic matter.

SEE ALSO

- **KNOW YOUR SOIL** >> 12/13
- **CHOOSING COMPOST** >> 18/19

JARGON BUSTER

Topsoil is the uppermost layer of earth, and it is usually darker in color and concentrated in organic matter, moisture, and nutrients.

Subsoil is the soil lying immediately under topsoil. It is usually lighter in color, because it contains less organic matter than topsoil.

Increasing drainage in clay soils Incorporating large amounts of coarse organic matter, such as well-rotted manure or spent mushroom compost, into the top layer will increase drainage, and sand can help, too (see opposite). You can work clay soil earlier in the season if you keep it dry over winter under plastic sheeting. Acidic clay can be broken up by applying a top-dressing of garden lime in spring, but don't then use fertilizer because the two do not mix.

Improving fertility and moisture in sandy soil

Well-drained sandy soils can be cultivated all year round, but the depth of fertile topsoil that plants can root into may be quite thin. The underlying subsoil is often compacted and mixed with rock fragments. Try to avoid bringing this layer to the surface because it is less fertile. In late winter or early spring, add a layer of well-rotted manure, or spent mushroom or garden compost, at least 4 in (10 cm) deep. This functions as a mulch, sealing in winter moisture and making soils less susceptible to summer drought. It also increases fertility in the soil around the plants' roots.

A coarse sand—about 1/2 in (10 mm) in diameter is ideal

Add coarse sand to improve drainage If you have soggy or clay soil, adding coarse sand will increase the drainage by decreasing the moisture-holding capacity of your soil. Incorporate the sand to a shovel's depth and in large quantities. Sand is not expensive, but it is very heavy, so calculate how much you need and remember it is easy to add more at a later date. Ensure only clean horticultural sand is used to avoid salt contamination.

CHOOSING THE RIGHT
POTTING SOIL

There are four common kinds of potting soil, but how do you know which one you need? Which is the best for long-lived plants? What is the fuss about peat? Are peat-free soils any good? Here are the pros and cons.

KEY POINTS

- **Different brands of loam-based** potting soil vary in quality. Check reviews of brands in the gardening press.
- **Plants need feeding** after six weeks when using peat-based soils.
- **Coir-based potting soil** is not entirely "green"—it is peat-free, but has to be shipped thousands of miles at significant environmental cost.

SEE ALSO

- **COLORFUL CONTAINERS** >> 36/37
- **MAKE HANGING BASKETS** >> 38/39
- **SHRUBS IN POTS** >> 112/115

FROM SEED TO PLANT
Larger plants need good nutrition to grow and thrive, so for these plants look for potting soils that advertise added fertilizer. Seeds and seedlings do not require extra fertilizer until they are larger.

Loam-based potting soil retains water and nutrients well

Loam-based or soil-based potting mixes These include sterilized natural soil as a component. As such, the quality and fertility are variable. Typically, these products contain sufficient nutrients for three months of plant growth.

Heat treatment has eliminated pests, diseases, and weeds

Peat-based potting soils These include multi-purpose types for seeds and general potting. Either is best for short-term, one-season use. Peat products are lightweight and well aerated, and the lack of nutrients is easily compensated for by the use of slow-release fertilizers. If the peat dries out, it shrinks and can be difficult to rewet.

Peat-free potting soil As concern about peat-stripped habitats grows, sales of peat-free potting soil have increased. One of the least environmentally damaging substitutes for peat is made from recycled household waste. It is dark colored and heavy, and suitable for most garden and pot plant needs. It is inexpensive, and holds water and nutrients well.

Coir-based soil dries out quickly, so plants need to be watered more frequently

Coir-based potting soil Made from shredded coconut husks, coir is sold loose or in blocks; the latter need to be soaked for about 20 minutes before use. Since coir is low in nutrients, it is generally mixed with multi-purpose potting soil. You can add one-third coir-based potting soil to two-thirds multi-purpose potting soil to improve its nutritional value for plants. Use it for annual displays in containers where a lightweight compost is needed, such as window boxes and wall pots, or on balconies.

CHOOSING
HEALTHY PLANTS

When you have found a plant you like, give it a quick once-over to make sure it has potential. Try to slide the plant out of its pot and look for healthy white roots growing in the potting soil. Choose a plant with vigorous top-growth and plenty of buds.

KEY POINTS

- **Resist the urge** to buy plants on impulse, and instead take the time to choose a healthy, vigorous specimen.

- **Instead of looking** at stem length, look for lots of healthy buds to ensure you get the best from your new purchase.

- **Avoid plants** that have wilting or discolored foliage, as well as those with weeds growing out of the potting soil.

SEE ALSO

- **CHOOSING POTTING SOIL** >> 18/19
- **GROW PLANTS THAT LAST** >> 28/29

BALANCED GROWTH
Check that plants have an even spread of top-growth. Some plants have a "front" and "back" because nursery staff don't have time to keep turning them to the sun, and as a result the growth may be lopsided.

Check the roots Avoid plants with so much congested root growth that you can't see the soil, a problem known as "pot bound," and/or with a knot of roots protruding from the drainage holes. Cramped, restricted roots can result in poor top-growth.

Avoid plants that have wilting or discolored foliage

Reject plants with poor growth
If an established plant has poor growth, there's a good reason for it. It may come from weak stock, in which case it will never amount to much, or it may have been badly neglected (right). The fact that it has been well watered on the day you see it doesn't mean that it has been well watered in the preceding days, or that it hasn't been left lying on its side in a shady corner.

Big isn't always best It's very tempting to buy the largest or tallest plant available, but don't equate size with potential—that can be a waste of money. Look for a sturdy young plant with plenty of new shoots and buds as well as a healthy root system that will flourish.

Inspect your specimen When buying from a reputable garden center it's very unlikely that you will encounter plant problems. However, you can hold the plant up to the light and check both sides of the leaves and stem. Discolored leaves may be a sign of a nutrient deficiency or another ailment.

FLOWERS
& FOLIAGE

SOWING SEEDS
OUTDOORS

Many hardy annuals, such as California poppies (*Eschscholzia*), are best sown outside where they are to grow and flower. This avoids having to sow in pots and transplant, although not all seeds can be sown this way. Check the seed packet for advice.

YOU WILL NEED

- seeds of hardy annuals, e.g., California poppies (*Eschscholzia*)
- fork
- rake
- cane
- watering can with fine spray nozzle

SEE ALSO

- **SOWING SEEDS INDOORS** >> 26/27
- **GROW PLANTS THAT LAST** >> 28/29
- **SEEDS IN POTS** >> 178/179

JARGON BUSTER

Annuals are plants that complete their life cycle (flowering, setting seed, and dying) within one year.

Hardy annuals withstand frost and cold and so can grow outside all year.

Half-hardy annuals are killed by frost and so are usually sown under cover then transplanted outside.

1 Select an open area without any competing plants for sowing the seeds. Lightly fork over the soil, breaking up large clods, and then remove large stones, weeds, and debris with a rake. Work the soil until it is fine and level.

3 Place the seeds into the palm of your hand, and aim to pour the seed gently from a crease as you pass your hand along the drill. Do not sow the seed too thickly. Larger seeds can be placed in the drill with your fingertips.

2 Make drills (shallow depressions to sow seed into) in the soil by pushing a pole or bamboo cane into the soil surface. Drills make it easier to identify your seedlings; weed seedlings are unlikely to emerge in straight lines.

4 Lightly cover the drills with fine soil, and water well using a can with a fine spray nozzle to avoid disturbing the seeds. Keep the seedbed moist and remove any weeds. When the seedlings emerge, carefully thin out close-growing plants.

SOWING
SEEDS INDOORS

While many short-lived plants can be sown outside in the garden, sowing seeds under cover gives plants an earlier start and often produces better results. Seeds can be sown in pots in a greenhouse, in a cold frame (a box with a glazed lid), or on a sunny windowsill.

YOU WILL NEED

- seed packets, e.g., nasturtium, pansies, chrysanthemum, or love-in-a-mist
- seed-starting potting soil
- 3½in (9 cm) plant pots
- watering can with fine spray nozzle
- small tray
- plant labels
- waterproof pen

SEE ALSO

- **SOWING SEEDS OUTDOORS** >> 24/25
- **GROW PLANTS THAT LAST** >> 28/29

LABEL YOUR POTS
Always write a label for your seeds using a waterproof pen. Include the name of the plant and the date of sowing so you don't forget. It can be fun at the end of the season to collect seeds for free from the garden.

Buy a fine, low-nutrient potting soil to grow seeds

1 Fill a clean or new 3½in (9 cm) pot with a good-quality seed-starting soil, leaving a ¾–1¼in (2–3 cm) gap beneath the rim of the pot. Firm the potting soil gently to create an even surface for the seeds.

2 Using a watering can with a fine spray nozzle, dampen the potting soil, being careful not to disturb it by splashing too much. Alternatively, stand the pots in a tray of water until the surface is moist, then remove to allow them to drain off.

3 Sow seed evenly, but don't over sow because thinning out excess seedlings will be difficult. A couple of large seeds per pot or a light sprinkling of small seeds is enough, covered with a fine layer of potting soil if instructed on the seed packet.

4 When the seeds have developed and produced a few sets of leaves, get them accustomed to being outdoors by placing the pots outside during the day for a few weeks. You can then plant them out in the garden.

GROWING
PLANTS THAT LAST

Perennial plants are the foundation of planning a great garden, often filling beds and borders. It is worth taking a little extra care at the start so these plants grow and establish well as they mature.

YOU WILL NEED

- 6½in (17 cm) potted plant, mint is shown here
- spade
- watering can
- garden compost

SEE ALSO

- **MAKING A BORDER** >> 44/47
- **RAISED BEDS AND EDGES** >> 50/53
- **CHOOSING FLOWERS** >> 54/57

JARGON BUSTER

Perennials are plants that live for more than two years, and may in fact live for many more years than that. They grow back each spring or summer from roots that go dormant in the soil over winter.

Herbaceous perennials are non-woody plants, unlike trees and shrubs, which are woody perennials. Herbaceous perennials typically flower for a certain amount of time in one season, unlike shorter-lived annual plants that may flower for much of spring and summer.

1 Place the plant in its pot on the ground to make sure you are happy with its position, before you go ahead and plant. The soil in the pot should be soaked before planting to give the plant a good start.

Make sure the spot chosen to plant is weed-free

3 Remove the plant carefully from its pot. If the roots are tightly packed around the root ball, the plant is pot-bound and the roots need to be teased out gently. Place the plant in the hole, slightly deeper in the ground than when it was in its pot.

2 With a spade, dig a hole wider and deeper than the size of the plant's container. Add organic matter, such as garden compost, to the base of the hole and dig it in well. Pour some water into the hole before planting.

4 Backfill soil around the roots, firming the earth as you go and ensuring the plant stands straight in its hole. Avoid raising the soil around the stems; the ground should be slightly sunken with the plant at the center. Water well.

GROWING
SUNFLOWERS

Bold and often extremely tall, sunflowers are one of the first flowers that many children recognize. They are fast-growing and are rewarding to grow from seed, often flowering into the fall.

YOU WILL NEED

- sunflower seeds
- 3$\frac{1}{2}$in (9 cm) pots (preferably biodegradable pots)
- seed-starting soil
- garden compost
- watering can
- plant food

SEE ALSO

GROWING STRONGER

Tie sunflowers to canes as they grow to keep them from being blown over. At a certain size, they should be self-supporting, although extra tall varieties may need a strong support. Water regularly for best results.

1 Fill a 3$\frac{1}{2}$in (9 cm) pot with seed-starting soil. Biodegradable pots, such as those made from coir fibers, are particularly useful because they can be planted directly into the ground, but seedlings will do just as well when grown in plastic pots.

2 Plant one seed per pot, pushing it just below the surface. Sow in spring indoors or in a heated greenhouse. Seeds can also be planted directly into the ground in late spring and early summer, but for the largest plants, start early.

Sunflowers grow very quickly from seed

3 Once the seeds have developed, keep the plants well watered. If you have started early, you may need to pot again into a larger pot while the plant is still indoors to keep it growing strongly.

4 When roots start showing through the bottom of the pot, put your seedling into a larger pot or out into the ground. When all danger of frost has passed, plant into ground that has been prepared with plenty of garden compost.

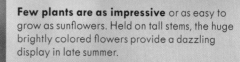

Few plants are as impressive or as easy to grow as sunflowers. Held on tall stems, the huge brightly colored flowers provide a dazzling display in late summer.

PREPARING POTS FOR **PLANTING**

All pots, large and small, need a few minutes' worth of preparation. Plants will live longer and look better if their pots are clean, with good drainage. Also consider the weight of your containers to avoid back-breaking lifting after planting.

KEY POINTS

- **As an extra precaution,** containers that previously held diseased plants can be soaked in baby bottle sterilizing solution.
- **Lining terra-cotta pots** prevents salts in the potting soil and water from leaching through the clay and discoloring the container.
- **Save money and potting soil** by filling up the bottom of the pot with polystyrene for short-lived displays.

SEE ALSO

- **CHOOSING POTTING SOIL** >> 18/19
- **COLORFUL CONTAINERS** >> 36/37

MOVING HEAVY POTS
It can be hard work to move large, full, heavy pots on your own. The best solution is to transport a container on a cart to avoid dropping it or hurting your back.

Check for drainage holes Most plant pots are made with drainage holes so excess water can drain away (if it can't, the plant will rot). If a pot doesn't have holes, you will need to make some. One way of doing this is to drill into the base several times with a masonry bit.

Small drainage holes allow less potting soil to fall out

Hammering holes You can either leave the drilled holes as they are, or tap them with a hammer to make one larger drainage hole. Choose clay containers with a thick base, which is less likely to fracture when hit with a hammer.

Alternatively, use ceramic balls instead of polystyrene

Stop the rot To help water drain freely, place broken pieces of pots or polystyrene at the base. Alternatively, use a layer of fine mesh with gravel on top. This prevents drainage holes from becoming blocked and potting soil from being flushed out.

Lighten the load Pots are heavy when filled with potting soil, and even heavier after being watered. To reduce the weight, fill the bottom third with polystyrene chunks. This is best for short-lived displays or plants that don't have long roots.

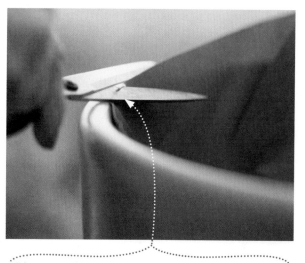

Re-use old pots It is a good idea to clean all pots, including those left in the garden or stacked up in the garage, immediately before use. This applies even if the pots were stored under cover and cleaned months ago before being put away. Undisturbed pots can be breeding grounds for pests and diseases, larvae, and baby slugs. Scrub with detergent and rinse well.

Line pots Clay pots that have not been glazed on the inside are vulnerable to frost damage. To prevent this, line pots that you want to sit outside all year with heavy-duty plastic. Push it well down into the pot, and use a pair of scissors to cut out drainage holes in the bottom. When the pot has been planted up, trim away the excess liner flush with the top of the container.

PLANT UP A COLORFUL
CONTAINER

One of the simplest ways of bringing a luxuriant display of seasonal color into your garden is to plant up a few pots. Follow these easy guidelines to help ensure that your displays are attractive and long lasting.

YOU WILL NEED

- potted plants, such as verbena and petunias, and trailing leaves like ivy
- large container
- potting soil
- water-retaining crystals
- gravel mulch
- watering can

SEE ALSO

- **CHOOSING POTTING SOIL** >> 18/19
- **PREPARING POTS** >> 34/35
- **CHOOSING FLOWERS** >> 54/57

JARGON BUSTER

Mulches are added around the plants in containers and beds.

They can be biodegradable (e.g., garden compost or bark chips) or non-biodegradable (e.g., gravel or sea shells). Mulches are used to help prevent moisture loss from soil and to suppress weeds.

Water-retaining crystals mean less watering for container plants

1 Before you plant the container, add water-retaining crystals to the potting soil. These swell up once moist, and provide plants with an extra reservoir of water, which helps ensure that they do not suffer during dry spells.

2 Arrange your selected plants in their original pots in the container to see how they look— this way, adjustments can be easily made. When you are satisfied, remove the plants from their pots and plant up the container.

3 Fill around the plants with potting soil when they are in their final positions, and ensure you leave a 2in (5cm) gap between the top of the soil and the rim of the container, to allow for easy watering and a layer of gravel.

Firm the soil gently so it is level with the plants

4 Spread a ³⁄₄in (2cm) deep gravel layer over the top of the potting soil as a mulch to conserve moisture in summer, deter weeds, and prevent unsightly debris splash when watering. It makes an attractive finish to the planting.

MAKE A SPRING
HANGING BASKET

Seasonal hanging baskets are easy to put together, and can vary from the delicate and subtle to the big and chaotic. Plant the dominant plants on top and decorative trailers around the sides.

YOU WILL NEED

- pot plants, e.g., skimmia, cyclamen, heathers, and pansies
- hanging basket
- basket liner or peat moss
- polythene liner
- wide short pot and small plastic pot
- multi-purpose potting soil
- water-retaining crystals
- newspaper and scissors

SEE ALSO

- **COLORFUL CONTAINERS** >> 36/37
- **CHOOSING FLOWERS** >> 54/57

JARGON BUSTER

Peat moss, also known as sphagnum moss, is found in wet places like peat bogs and marshes. It is comprised of fibrous material that occurs when mosses begin to slowly decompose away from air. Peat moss soaks up water like a sponge and can retain moisture during dry spells.

1 Stand the hanging basket on a wide, short pot to keep it stable during preparation. Line the basket with a coir basket liner, or use peat moss and pack it in tightly to a minimum thickness of 1¼in (3 cm).

2 Lay a circle of polythene at the base to help retain water. Cut holes in the liner, about 2 in (5 cm) above the base for trailing plants. Fill the basket to that level with potting soil mixed with water-retaining crystals.

Push trailing plants through a slit until the roots just rest inside the liner

3 Wrap paper around the root ball of each trailing plant (like this ivy) to protect it, and gently insert through a hole. The roots should be level with the soil in the basket. Add extra soil and firm it around the plants.

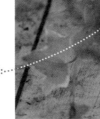

4 Put a small plastic pot near the center of the basket to act as a watering reservoir. Plant short plants at the edge of the basket, and tall ones in the center. Fill in around them with potting soil. Water the plants through the plastic pot.

PLANTING A
SHADY WINDOW BOX

You can bring color to a windowsill that receives little or no direct light with a well-planted window box. This one has been planned for summer interest with colors that glow in darker corners.

YOU WILL NEED

- shade-tolerant window box plants, e.g., artemisia, gypsophila, celosia, and fuchsia
- window box container
- gravel
- potting soil
- slow-release fertilizer

SEE ALSO

- **COLORFUL CONTAINERS** >> 36/37
- **MAKE HANGING BASKETS** >> 38/39
- **CHOOSING FLOWERS** >> 54/57

SALAD IN THE SHADE

Salad leaves, such as certain loose-leaf lettuces, can be grown in shadier spots. Lettuce leaves can be cut off for sandwiches or salads from the convenience of your kitchen window, and will regrow to yield more crops.

1 If necessary, make holes in the base of the container for drainage and cover the base with a light layer of gravel. Then add a layer of potting soil mixed with a slow-release fertilizer to give your new plants a head start.

Place upright plants in the middle and back rows of the box

2 Slide the plants from their containers and set them on the soil surface. Ensure that the top of the soil is 1 in (2.5 cm) below the rim of the box to allow for watering.

Don't add too much potting soil as it will spill over during watering

3 Fill around the plants with potting soil and firm it down. Put the box in position, then water well. Continue to water frequently throughout summer while the plants are in full growth. Cut off blooms as they fade, to prolong flowering.

PLANTING BULBS
IN A POT

Bulbs are easy to plant and grow well in a pot. A planting of mixed spring bulbs will give quick and colorful results. If you choose bulbs that flower at different times, the display will last longer.

YOU WILL NEED

- bulbs, e.g., tulips, daffodils, crocuses
- deep container
- broken pots or tiles
- gravel
- multi-purpose potting soil
- perlite

SEE ALSO

- **CHOOSING POTTING SOIL** >> 18/19
- **PREPARING POTS** >> 34/35
- **CHOOSING FLOWERS** >> 54/57

MORE FLOWERS

Choose some winter-flowering bedding plants to add on top of the bulbs in your pot. These will remain in flower as the bulbs are starting to push through the soil, then in spring the bulbs will become the main feature.

1 Choose a container with good drainage holes and then cover them with broken pots or tiles. These prevent the holes from getting clogged up with soil, which would stop water from draining away.

2 Some sun-loving bulbs, such as tulips, require really good drainage because they need to be kept fairly dry when dormant, and may rot if too wet. When planting these, add a layer of gravel to aid drainage further.

Gravel helps ensure the bulbs are not sitting in moist soil

3 Fill the pot with multi-purpose potting soil to within 6 in (15 cm) of the rim. Improve drainage by mixing in one part perlite (a type of volcanic glass) to every three parts of potting soil.

4 As a rule, bulbs should be planted at three times their own depth. Make sure the pointed shoot is facing upward. Then fill the pot with soil to within 2 in (5 cm) of the rim, to allow for easy watering.

MAKING A **BORDER**

Flower and shrub borders provide color, scent, and seasonal interest, making them an essential part of the garden. Follow these basic steps when planning and preparing your borders to ensure their success through the year.

YOU WILL NEED

- half-moon sod cutter
- garden hose (for a curved border)
- spade and fork
- soil rake
- well-rotted farmyard manure or garden compost
- sand or gravel
- wheelbarrow

SEE ALSO

- **RAISED BEDS AND EDGES** >> 50/53
- **CHOOSING FLOWERS** >> 54/57
- **CHOOSING SHRUBS** >> 140/143

LEFTOVER TURF

Leftover sod (see step 4) makes excellent compost, once the remaining grass has died off.

Alternatively, leave sod in a corner of the garden for wildlife such as mining bees to nest.

1 Decide where in the garden you want your border and mark out its shape. For a curved edge, use a garden hose. Make sure the border is not too narrow and that its shape suits the garden.

3 With a spade, begin stripping off the sod. Cut it into manageable squares from above, then slide the blade of the spade under the roots of the grass. Try to avoid removing an excessively deep layer of soil.

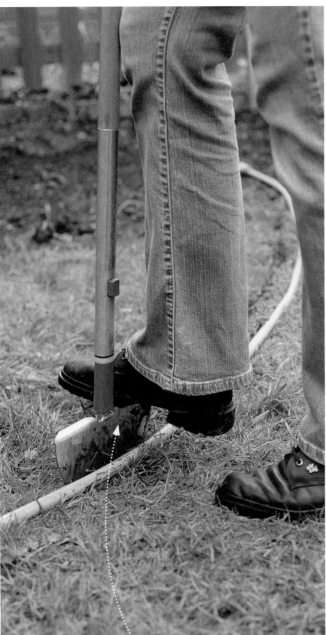

2 Using a half-moon sod cutter or a small spade, carefully slice through the grass, following the contours of the hose. Make sure the cuts align properly, and push the full depth of the cutter into the ground.

4 Stack the sod in a spare corner of the garden, grass-side down. The soil in this sod is nutrient-rich and should be reused. After several months, the grass will die off, and the pile can be cut up, sifted, and dug into the borders.

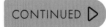 CONTINUED ▷

5 Dig over the exposed soil with a fork, pushing the sharp prongs down to their full depth. Remove old roots, large stones, and debris that you unearth, and break up large clods of soil. Work the soil until it has a crumbly texture.

6 With a spade, spread about 2 in (5 cm) of organic matter, such as well-rotted farmyard manure or garden compost, over the surface of the border. Turn the organic matter into the soil, and mix it in evenly.

7 If the soil is heavy or poorly drained, spread an 3 in (8 cm) layer of coarse sand or gravel over it, and dig this into the top 6 in (15 cm) of soil with a spade. This will help to open up drainage channels through the soil in the root zone.

8 Using a soil rake, remove any remaining stones, roots, or debris that may have worked their way up to the surface. Then, with the flat back of the rake, carefully level off any mounds and hollows.

Work the ground during spring or autumn when it is not too cold, hard, or wet

9 Set out the plants, still in their pots, on the ground, adjusting their positions until you are happy with them. Pay attention to their eventual size, flower and foliage color, and season of interest to achieve your desired effect.

VERBENA rigida

Keep plant labels as a reminder of what you have planted

Dahlias are excellent garden plants, giving a long-lasting late-summer display in the border or in containers. They come in an astonishing range of colors and shapes and make beautiful cut flowers.

MAKING RAISED
BEDS AND EDGES

A sturdy, timber-framed raised bed is quick and easy to construct, especially if the pieces are pre-cut to length at a timber yard. If your bed is adjacent to a lawn, finish it off neatly with a simple brick mowing edge.

YOU WILL NEED

- timber, e.g., softwood sleepers or reclaimed hardwood
- builder's spirit level, or plank of wood and short spirit level
- measuring tape
- rubber mallet and small trowel
- electric drill and lag screws
- broken bricks, concrete, or pottery

SEE ALSO

- **MAKING A BORDER** >> 44/47
- **LAWN EDGING** >> 64/65

WHAT TO PLANT
IN A RAISED BED

Raised beds can be used to plant aromatic herb gardens, mini fruit and vegetable patches, or simply for your favorite flowers. On clay soils, a raised bed will give improved drainage.

1 Dig out strips of sod wide enough to accommodate the timbers. Pressure-treated, softwood sleepers are an economical alternative to rot-resistant hardwoods like oak. You could also consider buying reclaimed hardwood.

2 Lay the timbers out in position and check that they are level using a builder's spirit level, or a plank of wood supporting a shorter spirit level. Check the levels diagonally between timbers, as well as along their length.

Treat wood with a preservative, if not already treated, to prolong its life outdoors

Position timber planks flush to one another

3 Ensure the base is square by checking that the diagonals are equal in length. For a perfect square or rectangular bed, it is a good idea to have the timbers pre-cut to size at a local timber yard.

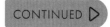

CONTINUED ▷

4 Using a rubber mallet, gently tap the wood so that it butts up against the adjacent piece; it should stand perfectly level and upright according to the readings on your spirit level.

Remove soil as necessary, to ensure the wood is level

5 Drill through the end timbers into the adjacent pieces at both the top and bottom to accommodate a couple of long, heavy-duty lag screws. Screw firmly into position, securing the base ready for the next level to be built.

6 Arrange the next set of timbers, making sure that these overlap the joints below to give the structure added strength. Check with a spirit level before screwing in the final set of fixings, as for step 5.

Remove any weeds from the plot

7 For the extra drainage required by tender plants, such as Mediterranean herbs, or alpines, part fill the base with broken pottery or masonry. Then add sifted topsoil that is guaranteed free from stubborn weeds.

CHOOSING FLOWERS AND FOLIAGE
FOR SPRING CONTAINERS

For a spring display, plan ahead and plant up your containers in fall. The plants selected here offer a range of shapes, sizes, and colors to combine. Some, such as the elephant's ears and heuchera, provide attractive winter foliage before the bulbs and other flowers burst into life.

ELEPHANT'S EARS
Bergenia 'Silberlicht'
Grow this evergreen perennial with spring bulbs in containers. It has large, oval, dark green leaves, which create a foil for the clusters of white flowers that appear on its red-tinged stems. It reaches about 18 in (45 cm) tall and its leaves spread slightly wider. It thrives in sun or partial shade and likes moist potting soil.

CROCUS
Crocus 'Snow Bunting'
Plant this corm (similar to a bulb) in small pots in fall for an early spring display. 'Snow Bunting' has fragrant white flowers with yellow centers and a purple blush on the outer petal surfaces. Its grasslike leaves are green with white lines. It likes a sunny spot in moist potting soil, and grows to 3 in (7 cm).

HEUCHERA
Heuchera villosa '**Palace Purple'**
This evergreen perennial has large, lobed, glossy, purple foliage, providing year-round interest. In a pot, its leaves are a foil for spring flowers, while in summer it produces small white flowers on wiry stems. Plant it in pots and place it in a sunny spot, keeping it well watered. It can grow to 18 in (45 cm).

GRAPE HYACINTH
Muscari armeniacum
Plant this spring bulb in autumn with daffodils and early tulips. The small, fragrant, deep blue flowers, held in cone-shaped clusters, are accompanied by grassy green leaves. It likes a sunny or partially shaded spot and well-drained soil, so avoid overwatering or ensure the pot drains effectively. It grows to 8 in (20 cm).

DAFFODIL
Narcissus '**Jack Snipe'**
Try combining this early to mid-spring–flowering bulb with grape hyacinth or polyanthus. It grows to about 9 in (23 cm) tall, producing creamy white flowers with short, bright yellow cups and narrow, dark green leaves. Plant in fall in a container of soil-based potting mix and set it in sun or partial shade.

ANGLED SOLOMON'S SEAL
Polygonatum odoratum
This perennial has oval to lance-shaped, mid-green leaves on arching stems and, in late spring to early summer, fragrant, hanging, bell-shaped, green-tipped white flowers. Plant it in containers in fall for spring color and fresh, substantial foliage. It can grow to 24 in (60 cm), and thrives in partial shade and when kept moist. Cut back in fall.

TULIP
Tulipa clusiana var. chrysantha
Blooming from early spring, this tulip makes a dainty feature in pots or troughs of well-drained, gritty, potting soil. It bears small, bowl-shaped, yellow blooms, tinged red on the outside. Plant the bulbs in fall, perhaps combined with blue hyacinths or scillas. It likes a sunny spot and may reach 12 in (30 cm).

PANSY
Viola x wittrockiana
This valuable short-lived plant has oval leaves and from late winter to spring produces flowers in almost every shade imaginable, providing a colorful frill around pots of spring bulbs. Plant it in containers of soil-based or multi-purpose potting mix in a sunny spot where it will bloom for many weeks before and while the bulbs flower. It reaches 8 in (20 cm).

CHOOSING FLOWERS AND FOLIAGE
FOR SUMMER CONTAINERS

If you spend time relaxing in your garden in summer, beautiful containers will give you a great deal of pleasure. A slow-release fertilizer mixed in at planting, combined with frequent watering and regular removal of fading blooms, will keep plants growing well for most of the summer.

SICILIAN CHAMOMILE
Anthemis punctata subsp. *cupaniana*

This evergreen, spreading perennial has silvery leaves and masses of daisylike summer blooms. Plant along with short-lived, colorful plants in mixed planters. Deadhead regularly to keep the flowers coming. It grows to 12 in (30 cm) and loves a sunny situation.

FERN-LEAVED BEGGAR-TICKS
Bidens ferulifolia

This annual plant's trailing stems of ferny green foliage and star-shaped, yellow flowers are perfect for edging tall pots or hanging baskets from summer to fall. Grow it in multi-purpose potting soil with pelargoniums or dwarf zinnias. It needs full sun and withstands drought well. It may grow to 12 in (30 cm) and spreads indefinitely.

COSMOS
Cosmos bipinnatus
Large, daisylike flowers in pink, red, and white make this short-lived plant a favorite for summer containers. The blooms are set off by soft, feathery foliage. Plant it in pots of multi-purpose potting soil, and deadhead to prolong flowering. Reaching a height of up to 4 ft (1.2 m), it needs a fairly large container and full sun.

DAHLIA
Dahlia 'Gallery Art Deco'
This decorative dahlia, which has double flowers with burgundy-edged pale orange petals, offers a splash of color in containers from midsummer to fall. Grow it in multi-purpose potting soil, and store the tubers in frost-free conditions over the winter. This plant likes a sheltered position in full sun and grows to 18 in (45 cm) tall.

HOSTA
Hosta 'Francee'
A showy perennial, 'Francee' has puckered green leaves, white-splashed around the edges, and pale blue summer flowers. It makes a great feature in a container in partial shade. Top the container with a gravel mulch to set off the leaves and retain moisture. Water well and shelter from damaging winds. This plant grows up to 2–3 ft (0.5–1 m).

HONEYBUSH
Melianthus major
One of the best architectural plants, the honeybush has large, toothed, gray-green leaves. Plant it in a large container to provide a backdrop of green foliage. It will grow up to 4 ft (1.2 m) and likes to be kept moist. Provide sun and shelter; the latter is crucial in winter when the top-growth dies back. If severe frosts threaten, provide protective cover.

PELARGONIUM
Pelargonium 'Lord Bute'
An evergreen perennial plant if protected from frost, 'Lord Bute' is usually grown as an annual. It has deep purple-red blooms throughout summer, set against rounded, hairy leaves. There are many other varieties to grow and all are ideal for window boxes and pots. Plant in multi-purpose potting soil.

SALVIA
Salvia patens 'Patio Deep Blue'
The flowers of this rich, blue perennial have an open mouth and are borne on tall spikes, reaching about 24 in (60 cm). It thrives in full sun and makes an elegant addition to a pot. Give it a sheltered location, water and feed it well, and deadhead it to prolong flowering. Protect it over winter.

LAWNS

LAYING **SOD**

The beauty of laying sod is that it produces an instant lawn. It can be laid at most times of the year, but will need regular watering during spring and summer. Although it is more expensive than seed, it can be walked on only a few days after laying.

YOU WILL NEED

- sod—make sure you buy enough rolls to fill the size of your lawn
- wooden plank
- garden broom
- garden rake
- top-dressing soil
- watering can or hose with fine spray nozzle attachment

SEE ALSO

- **SOWING GRASS SEED** >> 62/63
- **LAWN EDGING** >> 64/65
- **LAWN CARE** >> 70/73

GETTING THE BEST FROM SOD

Buy sod only from a reputable garden center or supplier and lay it on the day of delivery. If left stacked it can dry out and the grass will not receive enough light, so it turns yellow.

A straight, neat path edge makes it easier to later trim the sod

1 Prepare the site thoroughly by weeding and raking, and ensure that the soil is level. Roll the sod out and, once it is in place, firmly press down with the back of a rake. If possible, lay the first row of sod along a straight edge such as a path.

2 Ensure the edges of all the sods are butted up close to each other and pressed down firmly to prevent them from drying out. The joints of each row should be staggered, a bit like brickwork, as this creates a more sturdy lawn.

Stand on a wooden plank to avoid damaging newly laid sod

3 Once the lawn is finished, use a stiff broom to brush a good-quality, top-dressing soil into any cracks. No top-dressing soil should be left on the surface.

Top-dressing soil helps to smooth out the surface of the lawn

4 Finally, give the lawn a good watering. Do this frequently over the next few days to draw the roots down into the soil and to help it establish. Once the lawn starts to root, it can have its first cut at the mower's maximum height.

SOWING
GRASS SEED

By far the cheapest method of creating a lawn is sowing it from seed. The best time to sow is in spring or early fall. Seed can be sown in the summer but will need watering regularly; in winter, temperatures are usually too cold for the seed to germinate.

YOU WILL NEED

- grass seed
- canes and/or string
- garden fork
- garden rake
- seed spreader (optional)
- plastic sheet
- watering can or hose with fine spray nozzle

SEE ALSO

- **LAYING SOD** >> 60/61
- **LAWN EDGING** >> 64/65
- **LAWN CARE** >> 70/73

JARGON BUSTER

Germination is the process by which a seed starts to develop into a new young plant. For germination to happen, certain conditions need to be right, which vary according to the type of seed.

In simple terms, a seed needs the right temperature and some moisture to sprout and grow.

1 Prepare the area to be sown and then divide it into 3 ft (1 m) squares using canes or string. Measure out the amount of seed required per square foot as per the supplier's instructions.

Weed, level, and rake the soil before sowing

2 Sow the measured seed by hand. Half of the
seed should be spread in one direction and
the other half at 90 degrees to this. Ensure that
the seed is distributed as evenly as possible for
the best results.

Lay a sheet to
get neat edges

3 Rake the seed in gently. It should
ideally be covered by ¹⁄₁₆in (1–2mm)
of soil, although it can start to grow on
the surface. Water using a can or hose
with a fine spray nozzle. Grass will start
to emerge in one to two weeks.

An alternative to hand sowing is to
use a seed spreader, which is ideal if
you have a large area of ground to cover.
It will need to be calibrated to your
walking speed so it distributes seed at
the correct rate.

HOW TO MAKE
A **LAWN EDGING**

It isn't essential to use edging around a lawn, but it does make a neater, more distinctive feature of both grass and border and reduces the chore of keeping the edges neat.

YOU WILL NEED

- wooden edging
- half-moon cutter
- garden string
- hammer or rubber mallet
- spare piece of wood

SEE ALSO

- **RAISED BEDS AND EDGES** >> 50/53
- **MAKING A BORDER** >> 44/47

TREAT
WOODEN EDGING

Wooden edging should be painted or treated with a wood preservative to prevent it rotting. Do this 24 hours prior to inserting the edging panels into the ground.

Mow the lawn, if needed, before you start, to make the job easier

1 Peg a line of string taut along the desired edge and use a half-moon cutter to create a groove in the sod to a depth of about 3 in (7 cm). Remove any excess sod and push back some of the soil so it will be easier to insert the edging.

ALTERNATIVES

Wide brick edge Laid flat, bricks give a lovely finish to a lawn. When laid beneath the level of the sod, they make an ideal mowing edge.

Brick diamonds In brick diamond edging, bricks are laid diagonally with about half of the brick in the soil and the remainder above ground.

Victorian-style stone This style of edging looks good in the gardens of Victorian town houses where it will complement the architecture.

2 Place the sections of wooden edging over the groove and lightly tap them down using a hammer or rubber mallet. Place a piece of wood between the hammer and the edging to avoid damaging it.

Providing a restful green area or perhaps a play space, a lawn is often an integral part of an outdoor space. Its shape will reflect the design of the garden, with formal lines or sweeping curves.

GROWING BULBS
IN GRASS

Bulbs create a spectacular splash of color on the lawn. Most bulbs, including crocuses and scillas, are planted in the fall to bloom in spring, but with careful planning you can grow flowers in the lawn all year round.

YOU WILL NEED

- bulbs, e.g., daffodil or anemone
- bulb planter
- half-moon sod cutter or spade
- gravel or sand
- garden rake
- watering can or hose with fine spray nozzle

SEE ALSO

- **LAYING SOD** >> 60/61
- **SOWING GRASS SEED** >> 62/63
- **LAWN CARE** >> 70/73

DEADHEAD FLOWERS

Deadhead after flowering and leave for a few weeks until the foliage has died back, allowing nutrients to return to the bulb. Mow the faded foliage and give the lawn a light rolling to level it.

1 To make the planting look natural, scatter the bulbs across the lawn and plant them where they land. Use a bulb planter to take out a core of soil; bulbs should be planted at two to three times their depth.

2 If the soil is poorly drained, gravel or sand can be added. Place the bulb in the bottom of the hole with its growing tip facing upward. After planting, backfill the hole with soil and replace the plug of sod.

ALTERNATIVES

If you don't have a bulb planter, there is an alternative method of planting bulbs using a half-moon sod cutter or a spade. This is also a useful and quick technique to use if there are a lot of bulbs to plant, or if they are small and need to be planted close together.

1 Use a half-moon sod cutter or a spade to cut a square shape and then slice under the sod horizontally. Carefully peel the flaps of sod back. Lightly loosen the soil in the hole and add gravel or sand if the soil is poorly drained.

Avoid breaking up sod when peeling it back

Bulbs will push through the sod as they grow

2 Scatter the bulbs on the soil, ensuring that their placement looks natural. Plant them at the required depth, which is usually two to three times their height, with their growing tips facing upward.

3 Once the bulbs are planted, roll the sod back into place and make sure that they are completely covered. Firm the sod down well with the back of a rake, checking that the area is level with the rest of the lawn. Water well.

CARING FOR YOUR **LAWN**

Most lawns require little maintenance besides regular mowing, but to keep a lawn looking really good, it will need occasional attention. Tasks such as feeding and de-thatching will ensure that the grass stays healthy and lush.

KEY POINTS

- **In spring** the grass starts to grow as temperatures rise. Give a spring feed, and de-thatch lightly. Start to cut the lawn at a high level.
- **Summer** calls for regular mowing, and for watering only if needed.
- **Fall care** ensures the lawn survives the cold of winter. Feed, top-dress, de-thatch, and aerate it.

SEE ALSO

- **LAYING SOD** >> 60/61
- **SOWING GRASS SEED** >> 62/63
- **MAKE COMPOST** >> 234/235

WATER WISELY

Lawns only really need watering in extremely dry conditions. A well-maintained lawn will recover quickly after a period of drought. If you must water, then do so in the early morning or evening to reduce evaporation.

Feeding The three vital ingredients in a mineral fertilizer for your lawn are nitrogen (N), phosphorus (P), and potassium (K). Nitrogen promotes rapid leafy growth and is found in high quantities in spring feeds. Phosphorus promotes root growth, and potassium toughens up the grass; fall feeds often contain high levels of both. Feed at the rate recommended on the packet in spring and fall. You can also feed before sowing (shown here).

Watering In order to save time, large lawns are best irrigated with sprinklers, which can be timer-controlled to prevent water waste. There are various types available including oscillating sprinklers (shown here), which spray from side to side, and rotary arm sprinklers that spray the full 360 degrees. If you have a small lawn, you may want to use a hand-held wand with a spray attachment. Watering is essential when a lawn is newly laid or sown.

Avoid watering paths as this wastes water

Mowing Regular mowing encourages healthy new growth and a strong root system. It also deters weeds from seeding in the lawn. Different types of mowers are available, and some collect grass clippings as they go. Mowers can be gasoline driven, run on batteries, or push-propelled. They can be set to cut the lawn at different heights.

Weeding A few weeds are acceptable in a lawn, especially if they attract bees and butterflies. However, it is important to tackle those such as buttercups and dandelions that might take over a lawn or self-seed into borders. Weed by hand, prizing out the roots of persistent weeds.

CONTINUED ▷
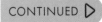

De-thatching Use a leaf rake to rip the "thatch" out of a lawn—the build-up of dead grass and clippings that can start to smother a lawn if left unchecked. De-thatch lightly in spring, and much more vigorously in fall. The best method in fall is to de-thatch in one direction and then again at right angles. The lawn can look much thinner afterward, but more light and air can now circulate among the grass. Compost the removed thatch.

Aerating Every spring and fall aim to aerate the lawn to relieve compaction. Spike the lawn at 4 in (10 cm) intervals with a fork pushed down to about 3–4 in (8–10 cm), wiggling the fork back and forth slightly to widen the holes.

Top-dressing will fill the holes created by aerating

Spread top-dressing evenly.

Brush in the top-dressing well so that it does not smother the grass

Brush into the lawn surface.

Top-dressing Applying top-dressing to your lawn improves the quality of the soil, levels out surface bumps and hollows, and fills the holes created by aeration. Ready-made mixes are available but you can make your own using sand, loam, and organic matter at a ratio of 3:3:1. Spread the top-dressing evenly across the lawn and then brush it into aeration holes using a broom. Ideally you should top-dress your lawn annually in fall.

Replacing a square of sod If a small area is damaged, cut out a square around the damaged part, lift it out with a spade, and dig over the base of the hole. Insert a square of sod the same size, pressing it down with the back of a rake. Water in well until it is established.

Raking leaves Use a leaf rake to collect leaves into piles. If left, the leaves will damage the grass by depriving it of light. The gathered leaves can be shredded with a lawn mower and then put on the compost heap or made into a pile to become leaf mold.

CLIMBERS

PLANTING
A **CLIMBER**

Climbing plants are particularly useful in small gardens because they add height and interest without taking up too much precious space. They are also a quick and effective way of covering dull walls and fences, and many have pretty foliage and flowers.

YOU WILL NEED

- climbing plants, e.g., clematis, wisteria, honeysuckle, or jasmine
- garden compost
- bark shreds
- canes
- twine
- spade
- trowel
- watering can

SEE ALSO

- **TOWER OF CLIMBERS** >> 82/83
- **CHOOSING CLIMBERS** >> 104/107

USING VINE EYES

A system of vine eyes (a type of screw) threaded with wire along a fence is the simplest and least visible way of providing support for climbers. The system is easy to attach and allows plants to grow to their full potential

1 Dig a hole twice the diameter of the root ball of the plant, 12–16 in (30–40 cm) from the fence. To support the stems and achieve good initial coverage, construct a fan from canes pushed into the soil and angled toward the fence.

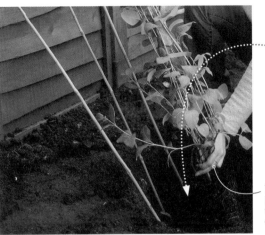

2 Make sure the plant is well watered, then position it in the hole at an angle pointing toward the fence. Carefully remove the pot and any supporting stakes. Untangle stems growing from the base (in this case a honeysuckle).

The hole should be just deep enough to fit the root ball of the plant

3 Backfill the hole with the removed soil mixed with some organic matter, such as garden compost. Firm the soil gently as you go. The ground around the plant should be slightly sunken to aid watering and to help the plant develop well.

Avoid stems tangling too much around each other

4 Select the stems to be trained up the canes, tying in one to two stems per cane with twine. Spread a layer of bark shreds or other organic matter, such as more compost, over the soil to keep in the moisture and suppress weeds.

POTTING UP
CLIMBERS

Well suited to growing in pots, all climbers need is a firm support and plenty of time to settle in. A feature can be made of the support—one that is elegant or attractively made will add to the display.

YOU WILL NEED

- a large pot or container
- wooden trellis support
- climbing plant, e.g., climbing rose
- broken pots or polystyrene pieces
- potting soil
- twine
- fine gravel
- hose or watering can with a fine spray nozzle

SEE ALSO

- **TOWER OF CLIMBERS** >>82/83
- **CHOOSING CLIMBERS**>> 104/107

JARGON BUSTER

A **trellis support** is a simple, flat framework of vertical supports with horizontal cross pieces, and is usually made of wood or metal. It can be plain or highly decorative.

You can make a trellis yourself or buy one from the garden center.

Make sure the trellis leaves enough room for the plant roots to spread out

1 Add a layer of potting soil, and then position the trellis support toward the back of the container, as shown above. To reduce the weight of the container, chunks of polystyrene can be added first, before the soil.

3 Fill around the plant with soil and lightly firm it with your hand. Ensure there is a gap of 2 in (5 cm) from the soil to the rim of the pot. Then fan out the stems and tie each one to the support with soft garden twine.

2 Part-fill the pot with more soil and sit the climber on top, to check that it will be at the correct level once planted. Remove the plant from its pot and place it on top of the soil, with the stems angled toward the trellis.

4 Add a layer of gravel or stones around the plant on the surface of the soil for decoration and also to help keep the climber's roots moist. Then water the plant in well using a hose or watering can with a fine spray nozzle.

PLANTING
AN **OBELISK**

Adding instant height and structure to a garden, an obelisk is particularly welcome in a bed planted mainly with low- to medium-growing plants. It is also a lovely way to show off climbers.

YOU WILL NEED

- obelisk climbing frame
- climbing plant, e.g., climbing rose
- garden compost
- twine
- watering can
- low-growing plants for the base, e.g., geraniums (optional)

SEE ALSO

- **PLANTING CLIMBERS** >> 76/77
- **POTTING UP CLIMBERS** >> 78/79
- **CHOOSING CLIMBERS** >> 104/107

FIGURE EIGHT TWINE

Many climbers need help to stay attached to their support. Use a soft garden twine and tie it in a figure eight to prevent the stem from rubbing against the obelisk structure.

1 Position your obelisk on an area of bare soil and push firmly into the ground. Placed on the corner of a bed it will be prominent and dramatic, while further back it creates height and therefore interest.

Any weeds should be removed before planting an obelisk

2 Dig a hole a short distance from the structure, larger than the plant's pot. Add compost to the base of the hole, then position the plant, leaning it inward toward the obelisk. Backfill with soil, firm in place, and water in well.

Plants that thrive in partial shade are a good choice for the base

3 Spread out the stems and tie them to the obelisk, but not too tightly. Most climbing plants will do the job of growing up the obelisk themselves. Watch at the start that stems don't stray, and later on prune or tie up wayward stems.

4 To soften the impact of the new structure, plant around its base. You can mix bedding plants, which flower for a long time in spring and summer but then die off, with perennial plants, which flower for a shorter time but come back year after year.

CREATE A
TOWER OF CLIMBERS

Some feature plants are best grown in pots where they are much easier to view and to care for, and you can stand them center stage when they are at their best. These morning glories (*Ipomoea purpurea*) grow very quickly from seed sown in the spring.

YOU WILL NEED

- 8 morning glory seedlings
- canes, or old stems, such as stripped forsythia, and twigs
- garden string or raffia
- small trowel or spoon
- multi-purpose potting soil
- watering can

SEE ALSO

- **POTTING UP CLIMBERS** >> 78/79
- **PLANTING OBELISKS** >> 80/81
- **CHOOSING CLIMBERS** >> 104/107

SUNNY CONDITIONS

Climbing morning glories come in many colors, including the intense, rich purple shown here. This tall plant likes sun, but can be damaged if the sun is too fierce; a spot with afternoon and evening sun is ideal.

Find old, hard tall stems or sticks for a wigwam

1 Arrange a wigwam of canes or old stems, such as stripped forsythia, around the edge of a container filled with potting soil. The wigwam doesn't need to be very neat—the stems will soon be obscured by the climbing plants.

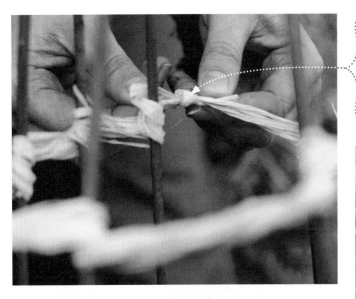

2 Tie the tops of the stems together. Then wrap string or raffia around the canes, about halfway up, to strengthen it. After planting, add more at different heights to make it easier for the climbers to spread across the frame.

3 Make planting holes by each support with a trowel or spoon. Remove the seedlings carefully from their pots. Gently prize apart the plants, handling them by their leaves, not the delicate stems. Plant one in each hole.

4 Firm all the plants in the soil, then water well. You may find it necessary to add an extra circle of twigs to help train the climbers onto the canes, and to stop them from climbing in the wrong direction.

MAKE AN
IVY TOPIARY BALL

A simple project for your garden is to create an "instant" topiary sculpture using ivy and a purpose-made frame. Here, an "ivy lollipop" has been created in a large plant pot in just a few easy steps.

YOU WILL NEED

- 3 ivy plants
- 2 wire hanging baskets
- plastic-coated garden wire
- wooden pole 4 ft (1.2 m) long
- 2 short pieces of wood
- hammer and nails
- large container
- terra-cotta or polystyrene pieces
- multi-purpose potting soil

SEE ALSO

- **TOWER OF CLIMBERS** >> 82/83

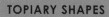

TOPIARY SHAPES

Buy different topiary shapes—such as topiary animals and tall abstract structures—from garden centers or online, or make them yourself for more interesting foliage in the garden.

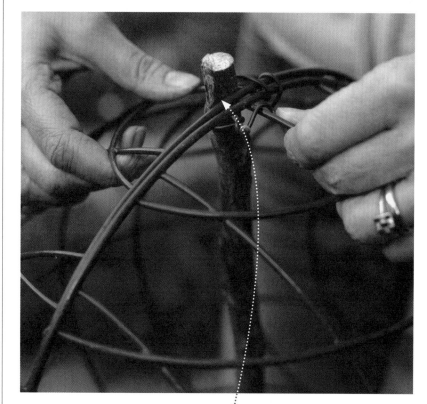

1 Use plastic-coated garden wire to fasten two wire hanging baskets together to form the shape of a ball. Suspend the ball from a nail driven into a sturdy wooden pole 4 ft (1.2 m) long. Use more wire to hold it in position.

2 Stand the pole with the attached "ball" in your chosen container and secure it with wire to a wooden, cross-shaped wedge fitted near the pot rim. Ensure the pole is kept perfectly vertical.

Nail two pieces of wood together as a cross and brace horizontally in the pot to support the stem

3 Place a layer of broken terra-cotta or polystyrene pieces in the bottom of the pot and fill it up with multi-purpose potting soil. Plant three ivy plants around the central pole and water in well.

4 Help the ivy climb by tying stems to the pole with garden twine. Once they reach the hanging basket ball, weave the stems in and out so they cover the surface. Once established, trim regularly to maintain the shape.

Clematis are perfect for concealing less attractive features, such as a bare fence, a wall, or a shed, with their leaves and attractive blooms. They also add height and color to your garden.

BUILD A
ROSE ARCH

A garden arch is the perfect framework for your favorite climbing roses. Other flowering climbers can also be trained over it to extend and diversify the display, to allow their perfumes to intermingle, and to create a more beautiful focal point.

YOU WILL NEED

- rose arch kit and a climbing rose
- tape measure
- spirit level
- screws (preferably galvanized)
- electric screwdriver
- spade and fork
- crusher run and ready-mix
- garden compost
- watering can

SEE ALSO

- **PRUNE A ROSE ARCH** >> 92/93
- **BARE-ROOT ROSE** >> 116/117

JARGON BUSTER

Crusher run is made of construction waste such as crushed rocks and gravel. It does not degrade easily and so makes a useful building base for outdoor structures.

Ready-mix is pre-mixed concrete that sets rapidly for installing wood, metal, and other structures in place.

1 Lay out the different pieces from the rose arch kit on the ground. Construct the top by aligning the five short cross pieces so that they slot into the two long cross beams. Use a tape measure to check they are evenly spaced.

2 Join the sections of the arch together using screws and an electric screwdriver. Galvanized screws are best for this because they do not rust, which ensures that your rose arch will last for many years to come.

Before drilling in screws, you can also pre-drill narrow holes to prevent wood splitting

You can buy crusher run online or from a builders' merchant

3 Stand the completed rose arch in its final position and mark out where the four uprights touch the soil. With a spade, dig four holes for the legs, 18 in (45 cm) deep and approximately 12 in (30 cm) in diameter.

4 Pour some crusher run into each hole to make a solid base for the legs to stand on. A depth of about 2 in (5 cm) will be sufficient. Tamp it down with a length of wood to make sure that it is level and firm.

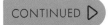

CONTINUED ▷

5 With help, lift the completed rose arch into place, lowering it into the holes. Make sure that each leg is standing on its base. Add or remove crusher run as needed until all legs are solidly supported.

6 Use a spirit level to make sure that all verticals are correctly aligned and that all horizontal pieces of the arch are level. If necessary, gently maneuver the structure until you are happy with its position.

7 To each hole, add some more crusher run. In a wheelbarrow, mix water and ready-mix according to the package directions.

8 Add ready-mix to fill the hole up to ground level. Ensure that the ready-mix completely surrounds the legs by pushing it into place with a gloved hand or a piece of wood. Allow the concrete to set and harden.

Work on a dry, clear day to allow the foundations to properly set

9 When the concrete has set hard, you are ready to plant some roses. Dig a hole 12in (30cm) away from the outside edge of one of the posts. Place your rose, still in its pot, into the hole and use a cane to check the planting depth.

Once the hole is filled, firmly press in soil with your feet

10 Mix some garden compost with the soil you have removed from the hole. Take the rose out of its pot and place it in the hole at 45 degrees to the arch. Plant it about 1in (2.5cm) deeper than the knobbly grafting point on the stem.

11 Fill in the planting hole with the compost and soil mix. It is important that there are no air gaps around the roots, so make sure the soil is crumbly with no lumps, and water in as you backfill, to prevent air pockets. Mulch with well-rotted manure.

PRUNING A
ROSE ARCH

To enjoy a rose arch year after year, prune the long branches each autumn so that the plant does not overwhelm the support and so that passage through the arch remains unrestricted. Climbing roses respond well to pruning and will flower the following summer. Remember to wear gloves to protect against thorns.

YOU WILL NEED

- sharp pruners
- loppers or a pruning saw
- wire staples and hammer
- plastic ties or twine
- thick garden gloves
- thick long-sleeved shirt

SEE ALSO

- **BUILD A ROSE ARCH** >> 88/91
- **PRUNE A ROSE WALL** >> 94/95
- **BARE-ROOT ROSE** >> 116/117

CLEAR AWAY THE OLD

On well-established roses older wood can become unproductive, failing to produce new shoots and flowers in the growing season. Removing some of this thicker wood will allow new growth to take over.

1 In fall, first remove any dead, diseased, dying, or crossing stems, to ensure you are left with only the healthiest and strongest branches. Then you can start to prune the climber to the desired shape.

Unhealthy stems may appear peeling or cracked with scales or fungi

2 Armed with a pair of sharp pruners, cut each recently flowered stem back by about two-thirds to just above a strong, healthy bud. The cut should be made at an angle, so that rain will drain away from the bud.

Watch out for the adjacent thorny branches—wearing long sleeves is best

3 On an established climbing rose, remove old, unproductive stems close to the base using a pair of loppers or, ideally, a pruning saw to ensure a clean cut. This will stimulate the growth of new shoots.

4 Finally, tie in the pruned new growth to wire staples hammered firmly into the arch. Use adjustable plastic ties, as shown here, or garden twine fastened in a figure eight to support the stems securely.

PRUNING A
ROSE ON A WALL

Climbing roses will soon grow out of control if they are not pruned regularly. It is worth spending time each year removing unwanted stems and re-tying the remaining framework to its supports.

YOU WILL NEED

- pruners
- pruning saw
- twine
- well-rotted manure or garden compost
- thick garden gloves
- thick long-sleeved shirt
- ladder

SEE ALSO

- **PRUNE A ROSE ARCH** >> 92/93
- **CHOOSING CLIMBERS** >> 104/107
- **BARE-ROOT ROSE** >> 116/117

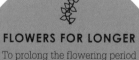

FLOWERS FOR LONGER

To prolong the flowering period of a climbing rose, deadhead the flowers as they fade by removing them with a pair of pruners. This encourages the plant to produce more blooms.

1 Before making any cuts, stand back and look at the rose growing against the wall, to visualize what it will look like after pruning. You will then know which stems to remove when you are closer to the climber.

Tie a knot of twine around stems to identify those to cut back

2 In fall or early winter, after flowering, cut out dead, diseased, or rubbing stems. Then remove any main stems that have outgrown their allotted space. Use a pair of pruners or a pruning saw if the branch is thick.

4 Reposition the main stems against the horizontal wire supports and tie them in using garden twine. You may need to hold them in position while tying, to prevent them crossing over other stems.

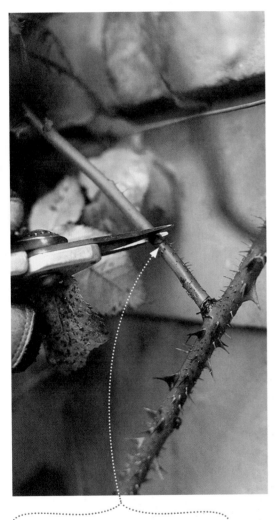

3 Shorten the remaining side shoots by up to two-thirds to two or three healthy buds. Always prune to just above an outward-facing bud, so that the new shoots are well positioned and grow away from, or adjacent to, the wall.

5 The end result should be an open framework. One stem here crosses others to fill a gap, but it isn't close enough to rub. Spread a layer of well-rotted manure or garden compost around the base to conserve moisture and to feed the plant.

A climbing rose is a versatile addition to the garden, and can be grown up walls and fences, as well as over an ornamental arch. Its prolific blooms and often deep fragrance are a summer highlight.

PRUNING
WISTERIA

There are few sights as glorious as a mature wisteria in full bloom, but wisterias can grow very large. Prune in summer to keep long, whippy growths in check, and again in winter to keep the plant to size and to encourage more flowering the following year.

YOU WILL NEED

- pruners
- twine
- garden gloves

SEE ALSO

- **PRUNE A ROSE ARCH** >> 92/93
- **PRUNE A ROSE WALL** >> 94/95
- **PRUNING KNOW-HOW** >> 236/237

PRUNE HARD

Prune stems that are climbing up vertical supports to encourage as many new flowers to grow as possible. Hard pruning involves significantly cutting back old stems and branches to rejuvenate the plant for spring.

Removing overgrowth allows more sunlight and air to reach new shoots

1 Left to its own devices, a wisteria will send out long, whippy stems, which by summer will become an unruly tangle. The plant will flower better the following year when pruned and trained flat against a wall or fence.

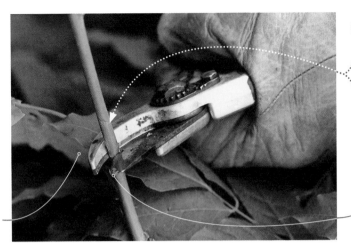

2 In late summer, about two months after flowering, prune the current year's stems back to 6 in (15 cm) from a main branch with a pair of pruners, leaving no more than six leaves. Be careful not to damage the buds.

Don't hurry when pruning, and find the right spot to cut back

Cut at a slight angle in the same direction as the buds

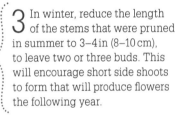

3 In winter, reduce the length of the stems that were pruned in summer to 3–4 in (8–10 cm), to leave two or three buds. This will encourage short side shoots to form that will produce flowers the following year.

4 It is important to prune the wisteria all over, leaving a framework of shortened stems. Make sure that long stems are tied in well to prevent these from breaking or being damaged in the wind.

CUTTING BACK **IVY**

Ivies are versatile evergreen climbers that will grow in sun or shade, and adhere to almost any support or surface. In late spring or early summer, prune these vigorous plants to contain their spread, and to prevent stems from growing into unwanted places.

YOU WILL NEED

- pruners
- dust mask
- garden gloves
- garden trash bag

SEE ALSO

- **IVY TOPIARY BALL** >> 84/85
- **PRUNING LIGHTLY** >> 120/121
- **PRUNING KNOW-HOW** >> 236/237

FALL IVY NECTAR

Avoid pruning ivy from late summer to early winter as this is often when the plant flowers. Ivy flowers provide a valuable late source of nectar for bees and other pollinating insects.

Ivy can block out sunlight for other plants as it climbs over walls, fences, and trees

1 The aim of pruning here is to reduce the plant's spread over the fence and to remove it from the tree trunk in front. Ivy can collect a lot of dust and dirt, so wear a dust mask when pruning if this affects you.

2 Working from the top of the fence panel, pull away long lengths of ivy. When you are happy with the amount removed, cut off the stems with pruners. Also cut and pull away any ivy growing on tree trunks or other plants.

3 Remove ivy growing up walls and into house guttering. When removing ivy from walls you will reveal marks left by the clinging roots. If you feel the need, use a stiff brush to remove the root residue.

4 The ivy has been cut back from the top of the fence by about 18 in (45 cm) to allow room for regrowth. It has also been removed from the tree trunk, resulting in a less cluttered and lighter part of the garden.

RAISE NEW PLANTS
BY LAYERING

Layering is a simple way of propagating plants by wounding a low-growing stem and keeping it in contact with the soil until roots form. This basic technique can be used for many climbers.

YOU WILL NEED

- climbing plant, e.g., chocolate vine, blue passion flower, crimson glory vine
- 4 in (10 cm) plant pot
- multi-purpose potting soil
- sharp, clean knife
- hormone rooting powder (optional)
- small piece of wire
- cane stick and string

SEE ALSO

- **GROW HERB CUTTINGS** >> 210/213

MORE LAYERING

Create more than one plant from each stem by adapting the method shown opposite. Make a series of wounds between the leaf joints of a stem, treat with hormone powder, and peg each wound just below the soil.

1 In spring, bury a 4 in (10 cm) pot almost to its rim in the soil close to the plant you want to layer. Fill it with fresh, multi-purpose potting soil and lightly firm with your fingers.

2 Take a healthy, low-growing stem and stretch it across the pot surface. With a sharp, clean knife make a nick in the underside of the stem, halfway between two sets of leaves.

Using hormone rooting powder is optional but increases the plant's chances of taking root

Tie the string loosely around the stem so as not to restrict its growth

3 Dip the exposed cut in some hormone rooting powder to help speed up the formation of roots. Remove any excess powder by gently tapping the stem with your fingers. Wash your hands after handling the rooting powder.

4 Bend a small piece of wire to form a "U" shape and place over the stem, pushing the cut below the surface of the soil. Cover with a little more soil if necessary.

5 Tie the free end of the stem to a cane support alongside the sunken pot. By fall, roots should have formed. Then sever the layer close to the parent plant using pruners, and cut the old stem on the layer back to the roots.

CHOOSING CLIMBERS
FOR SPRING INTEREST

Ideal for covering walls, fences, arches, and obelisks, the climbing plants and wall shrubs chosen here are particularly valuable in spring, adding colorful flowers and attractive foliage to the vertical surfaces of your garden just as the rest of the garden is coming back to life.

KOLOMIKTA
Actinidia kolomikta

A twining climber, kolomikta produces masses of purple-hued leaves that turn green, pink, and white. Full sun will bring out the different colors of the foliage. In early summer, kolomikta bears small clusters of lightly fragrant flowers. It can grow up to 15 ft (5 m), and prefers well-drained soil. Train the stems along wires against a wall.

ALPINE CLEMATIS
Clematis alpina

With divided, mid-green leaves, alpine clematis is deciduous and bears lantern-shaped, blue, pink, or white flowers, depending on the variety, from early to late spring. These are followed by fluffy, silvery seed heads. It can reach a height of 10 ft (3 m) and likes a well-drained soil. Keep the roots shaded.

MOUNTAIN CLEMATIS
Clematis montana
This vigorous, deciduous climber has divided, mid-green foliage. From late spring to early summer it produces an abundance of scented white or pale pink flowers with yellow centers. Provide a large support, such as a tree, wall, or pergola, as it can scramble to 40 ft (12 m) unchecked. It likes sun or partial shade and a moist but well-drained soil.

CHILEAN GLORY FLOWER
Eccremocarpus scaber
A fast-growing climber, this vine produces clusters of tube-shaped, orange-red flowers from late spring to fall. Chilean glory flower prefers well-drained sandy or loamy soils in sunny, sheltered sites. Grown up a trellis or obelisk, its clinging tendrils will achieve heights of 8–13 ft (2.5–4 m). Enjoy its dark-green foliage all year round.

WEEPING FORSYTHIA
Forsythia suspensa
With slender, arching stems and small, toothed, green leaves, weeping forsythia makes an excellent deciduous wall shrub. It is grown mainly for the nodding, narrow, slim-petaled, bright yellow flowers that form on its bare branches in early spring. It can reach 10 ft (3 m) and prefers a well-drained site. Prune after flowering.

ITALIAN JASMINE
Jasminum humile 'Revolutum'
An evergreen climbing shrub, Italian jasmine has glossy, bright green leaves, divided into leaflets, and fragrant, tubular, bright yellow clusters of flowers from early spring to early summer. 'Revolutum' is a popular and reliable variety. Grow it in a sheltered site on well-drained soil, where it can reach a height of 8 ft (2.5 m).

SCHISANDRA
Schisandra grandiflora
Delicate white flowers are borne on this twining deciduous climber from late spring to summer. If there is a male schisandra plant nearby, the female will also produce hanging red fruit in fall. It prefers a sheltered spot with moist but well-drained soil in sun or partial shade, where it will reach a height of 30 ft (10 m).

WISTERIA
Wisteria x formosa
This vigorous, twining, woody climber has a graceful appearance. In late spring and early summer, mauve-purple, pealike, fragrant flowers are produced, adding scent as well as color to the display. Furry, runner bean–like seed pods often form after flowering. Wisteria likes well-drained soil in sun or dappled shade, and will grow up to 30 ft (9 m).

CHOOSING CLIMBERS
FOR SUMMER INTEREST

Many climbing plants and wall shrubs like to have their roots in shade while their stems climb toward the sun. Those chosen here are at their best in summer, from the fragrant honeysuckle and roses, to black-eyed Susan, which makes a striking summer feature in a pot.

CLEMATIS
Clematis 'Jackmanii'

This colorful clematis is best grown around doorways and windows, where its abundance of large, purple flowers can be appreciated from mid- to late summer. It prefers full sun to partial shade, suits most soil types that are moist and well-draining, and reaches heights of 8–13 ft (2.5–4 m). Prune all the stems down to soil level in early spring.

CLIMBING HYDRANGEA
Hydrangea anomala subsp.
petiolaris

This vigorous, woody climber has broad, rounded leaves and produces large, open heads of creamy white flowers in summer. Young plants need support until they are established. Grow in sun or partial shade and moist but well-drained soil. Slow growing at first, it can reach 50 ft (15 m) but can be cut back.

HONEYSUCKLE
Lonicera periclymenum 'Serotina'
A highly fragrant honeysuckle, this grows vigorously through shrubs and trees, or over arches, up to 13–26 ft (4–8 m). It has lush foliage in spring and purple-streaked, white flowers in mid- to late summer; the scent is strongest in the evening. It prefers partial shade but will tolerate full sun and grows well when planted in moist, well-drained soil.

BLUE PASSIONFLOWER
Passiflora caerulea
This exotic-looking climber produces large, white flowers with purple, blue, and white filaments in summer. These are followed by oval, orange fruits. It is fast-growing in full sun or partial shade, and thrives in most moist, well-drained soils. It may be planted in borders along walls and fences, or in containers, and grows up to 26–39 ft (8–12 m).

RAMBLING ROSE
Rosa 'Albertine'
This rose provides a showy display of very fragrant, salmon-pink flowers in midsummer. It is a large and vigorous rambler that can be grown into trees or over structures, reaching up to 16 ft (5 m). Alternatively, train along a wall or fence. It likes a sunny spot, and moist, well-drained soil, but tolerates poor soils. Prune after flowering.

CLIMBING ROSE
Rosa 'Golden Showers'
From summer to fall this climber produces deeply fragrant, golden-yellow flowers against dark stems and glossy green foliage. 'Golden Showers' grows best in full sun and rich, moist, well-drained soil, but tolerates shade and poor soils. It grows to 8–13 ft (2.5–4 m). Plant along walls or fences in borders. Prune in late fall to early spring.

CHILEAN POTATO VINE
Solanum crispum 'Glasnevin'
A semi-evergreen, scrambling climber, the Chilean potato vine has oval green leaves and clusters of fragrant, yellow-eyed violet-blue flowers from summer to fall. These are followed by creamy white fruits that are toxic. Grow it in a warm, lightly shaded spot, where it can reach 20 ft (6 m). Tie in the stems regularly to keep it within bounds.

BLACK-EYED SUSAN
Thunbergia alata
Black-eyed Susan is a very decorative climber that may be grown for only one season for its bright orange-yellow blooms with distinctive black eyes. Plant in a large container, in moist, well-drained soil, and position it in a sunny spot, training it up a metal or wooden pyramid. This climber can grow up to a height of 8 ft (2.5 m).

SHRUBS

PLANTING
A **SHRUB**

Shrubs have an important place in any garden, providing rich texture as well as flowers and foliage. Before planting, check the plant label for the shrub's preferred site and soil, since moving it at a later date will be difficult.

YOU WILL NEED

- container-grown shrub, e.g., currant bush, shown here
- large spade
- large fork
- cane
- garden compost
- watering can

SEE ALSO

- **CHOOSE HEALTHY PLANTS** >> 20/21
- **BARE-ROOT ROSE** >> 116/117
- **CHOOSING SHRUBS** >> 140/143

FEED YOUR SHRUB
Once planted, apply a top-dressing of slow-release fertilizer above the roots. Later watering or rain will wash it down. This will give the shrub a boost during the growing season.

1 Soak the plant thoroughly in its pot. Dig a large hole, approximately two to three times the diameter of the pot. Remove any old roots and large stones, and break up the soil in the base of the hole with a fork.

A wide rather than deep hole is needed for a shrub

2 To check the hole is the correct depth, place a cane across the top; it should rest on both sides of the hole and on the top of the root ball. Position the plant with its best side facing the direction from which it will be viewed.

3 Remove the pot; it should slide off easily, leaving the root ball intact. Tease out any encircling roots. Add well-rotted organic matter, such as garden compost, to removed soil, especially if it is poor. Backfill around the root ball.

4 Water the plant well as you backfill the soil around the root ball. Firm the earth down gently. The earth surrounding the plant should be slightly sunken to assist watering. Spread a mulch of well-rotted organic matter, such as garden compost, around the plant, keeping it away from stems.

PLANTING A
SHRUB IN A POT

Evergreen shrubs, such as hebes, make beautiful ornamental features for small spaces when planted in pots. Buy a plant with healthy leaves and an attractive shape, and avoid those with lots of roots poking through the base of the container.

YOU WILL NEED

- evergreen shrub, such as hebe, shown here
- container with drainage holes
- broken flower pots (crocks) or polystyrene pieces
- potting soil (without peat)
- small-stone gravel
- watering can with fine spray nozzle

SEE ALSO

- **PLANT A SHRUB** >> 110/111
- **REPOTTING SHRUBS** >> 138/139
- **CHOOSING SHRUBS** >> 140/143

EVERGREEN SHRUBS

Shrubs that keep their leaves all year are known as evergreens. They provide year-round interest for small gardens where planting a tree may not be suitable. Many also produce colorful flowers followed by berries.

Choose a frost-proof container to keep shrubs outdoors in winter

1 First, check that the pot has drainage holes in the bottom, and drill a few if there are none. Place pieces of broken flower pots, or pieces of polystyrene—old plant trays are ideal—on the bottom to aid drainage. Do not block the holes.

2 Start filling the pot with fresh potting soil. If the soil is lumpy, break it up. Stop filling when you can stand the plant in its container on the soil with a 2 in (5 cm) gap to the rim of the pot.

Make sure the soil isn't too dry or wet

3 Place the shrub in its container in the center of the pot, and start filling around it, firming in the soil. The aim is to create a hole for the plant to slot into, in exactly the right place and at the right depth. If it's off-center, try again.

Plants prefer loose soil so don't firm it at this stage

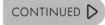

CONTINUED ▷

Lift the shrub slowly to keep its hole in the container intact

4 Gently lift the shrub in its container straight up and out of the pot, leaving the hole intact. If you haven't already done so, give the shrub a good drink and let the water drain away. This ensures the plant gets off to a good start.

5 Carefully remove the shrub from its container, taking care not to damage its roots or break off any top-growth. Then tease out the roots at the edge of the root ball to encourage them to grow outward.

6 Gently lower the shrub into the hole, and firm in the soil all around. Add a little more potting soil, if needed, to give a level surface, but make sure it is no higher up the stem than when the plant was in its original pot.

7 Water in the shrub to settle the soil and to remove any air pockets. If you don't have a fine spray nozzle, pour the water onto a broken piece of flower pot so it flows evenly and doesn't expose the roots. Repeat in each corner of the pot.

A layer of gravel helps deter weeds

8 As a final decorative touch, scatter gravel, shingle, or small pebbles in a thin layer around the shrub. Available in various colors, they set off the plant and help keep the soil moist by reducing evaporation.

PLANTING A
BARE-ROOT ROSE

Roses are essential shrubs for the garden and come in many varieties. Pot-grown roses can be planted all year round like other shrubs. Roses are also available bare-root, with no soil, for planting when dormant in winter.

YOU WILL NEED

- bare-root rose
- pruners
- thick gloves
- spade and fork
- cane
- mycorrhizal fungi (optional)

SEE ALSO

- **PLANT A SHRUB** >> 110/111
- **PRUNE SHRUB ROSES** >> 122/123
- **PRUNE A WALL ROSE** >> 94/95

JARGON BUSTER

Bare-root refers to plants dug out with the soil shaken off their roots and placed in moist packing material for sale and/or transport. They are only supplied in the winter months, and are mainly trees, shrubs, and hedging plants.

If you cannot plant a bare-root plant as soon as you receive it, heel it into the ground temporarily by planting it very roughly with soil covering the roots so it does not dry out or get frost damage.

1 Remove diseased or damaged growth. Cut out any crossing shoots and thin or straggly stems at the base to produce a balanced shape. Trim any thick roots by about one-third.

2 Dig out a hole with a spade, slightly wider and deeper than the roots of the rose. Use a fork to loosen the soil at the base. You can mix in mycorrhizal fungi, according to the packet instructions, to encourage healthy roots.

3 Place the rose in the center of the hole and spread out the roots evenly. Lay a cane across the hole to check that the bud union will be 1 in (2.5 cm) below soil level when the rose is planted, adjusting the depth if needed.

4 Fill in the hole with soil, firming with your hands in stages to anchor the roots firmly in the soil. Lightly tread down the surrounding soil. Gently rake over the soil and water well.

PRUNING AN EARLY
SUMMER FLOWERING SHRUB

For shrubs to perform at their best, they need an annual prune. Prune those that flower in early summer after flowering. Some need a light trim, while others, like this mock orange (*Philadelphus*), can be cut back harder to encourage new stems.

YOU WILL NEED

- pruners
- garden gloves
- garden waste bag

SEE ALSO

- **PRUNING WISTERIA** >> 98/99
- **PRUNING LIGHTLY** >> 120/121
- **PRUNING HYDRANGEA** >> 124/125

WHEN TO PRUNE

Shrubs that flower in early summer are best pruned after flowering. For those that flower later in the summer, prune in early spring so new stems can grow to flower later the same year. Avoid pruning in winter.

1 Wait until the flowers begin to fade before pruning. With annual pruning, this mock orange will continue to bear its masses of scented white flowers in early summer year after year.

2 Cut back about a quarter of the oldest flowering stems to 6 in (15 cm) above the ground. This encourages young, vigorous stems to grow from the buds below the pruning cuts, and these stems will bear next year's flowers.

3 Shorten any old stems that have young growths lower down. Take off the top third of these old stems, pruning them back to a younger branch. Also remove any dead, damaged, or diseased wood.

4 Trim the tips of any strong young stems that are already present to encourage lower branching and more flowers. The finished plant should look more compact and tidy, and give rise to lots of young, fresh growth.

LIGHTLY
PRUNING SHRUBS

Many shrubs, such as this *Daphne bholua* 'Jacqueline Postill,' produce long, leggy growths in the spring. Trim these and the resulting plant will be bushier with more flowers.

YOU WILL NEED

- pruners
- garden gloves
- garden waste bags

SEE ALSO

- **PRUNING SUMMER SHRUBS** >> 118/119
- **PRUNE SHRUB ROSES** >> 122/123
- **PRUNING KNOW-HOW** >> 236/237

PRUNING
YOUNG PLANTS

Where the growths are softer on young plants, pinch out the tips with your thumb and forefinger. This is good practice, because it helps to produce a compact, well-branched structure.

1 In early summer, *Daphne* starts to produce many long growths at the ends of its main stems. These can give the plant an untidy and leggy appearance.

2 Using pruners, shorten the leggy growths by 6–8 in (15–20 cm). Always prune immediately above a leaf bud with an angled, slanting cut, as shown.

Hold a branch firmly to help you to prune at an angle

Extra growth that is pruned out could be used for cuttings

3 Continue to work around the plant. Trimming the stems like this encourages bushier growth, and all the new stems will produce flowers in the winter. It also helps keep the plant smaller and more compact.

PRUNING A
SHRUB ROSE

Most modern shrub roses are repeat flowering and do not need to be pruned as hard as bush roses, since they flower on older stems. Prune your shrub roses in early spring.

YOU WILL NEED

- thick gloves
- pruners

SEE ALSO

- **BARE-ROOT ROSE** >> 116/117
- **PRUNE A ROSE ARCH** >> 92/93
- **PRUNE A ROSE WALL** >> 94/95

PRUNE BUSH ROSES

Prune Hybrid Tea and Floribunda bush roses hard in early spring. Cut out old, diseased, and crossing shoots and then cut the rest to 6in (15cm) from the ground for Hybrid Teas, 8–12in (20–30cm) for Floribundas.

1 The aim of pruning a shrub rose is to create a strong structure and to remove congested stems that were produced the previous year. This improves air flow through the plant, which helps prevent fungal diseases.

3 Reduce healthy main stems by a quarter, and prune some of the sideshoots by just a few inches (centimeters). Always cut above a healthy bud that faces outward, away from the center of the plant, if possible.

2 Cut off any dead, damaged, or diseased branches. Then remove any weak shoots that are not strong enough to support new flower growths. Also prune a few of the oldest stems down to the ground.

4 The pruned plant should be reduced in height by about a quarter, and have a strong, open, structure that appears uncluttered in the center. By midsummer the plant should be covered in beautiful blooms.

PRUNING
HYDRANGEA

Hydrangea macrophylla, or mophead hydrangea, flowers in summer from buds that have been set the previous year. Careful pruning will protect these developing buds, which are prone to frost damage in the spring, ensuring a good display of flowers.

YOU WILL NEED

- pruners
- garden gloves
- garden waste bags

SEE ALSO

- **PRUNE A ROSE ARCH** >> 92/93
- **PRUNING WISTERIA** >> 98/99
- **PRUNE WINTER STEMS** >> 130/131

COLOR CHANGES

Mophead hydrangea is one variety known to change flower color depending on the soil type: blue in acid, mauve in neutral, and pink in alkaline soils. White varieties stay white regardless of soil pH.

1 The hydrangea's old flower heads help protect the delicate new flower buds from frosts. Leave them on the plant during the winter to ensure a good display of colorful blooms the following summer.

2 When the danger of hard frost has passed in late spring, remove the flower heads by pruning the stems back to a pair of healthy buds, as shown.

Bare stems continue to add structure and interest to the winter garden even after the dried flowers are removed

3 Do not be tempted to prune too hard as this will remove many of the flower buds already formed on the stems that grew the previous year. New stems that grow in the coming year will bloom the following summer.

With their large, showy flowers, hydrangeas are shrubs that offer long-lasting interest. They bloom for weeks at a time, then their fading flower heads give structure in the border in winter.

PRUNING
LAVENDER

Lavender (*Lavandula*) is a beautiful aromatic shrub that can be grown on its own or as a low-growing, colorful hedge. To maintain a good shape, it is best pruned twice a year, with a thorough prune in spring, then deadheading after flowering.

YOU WILL NEED

- hedge clippers

SEE ALSO

- **LAVENDER HEDGE** >> 208/209
- **CHOOSING SHRUBS** >> 140/143

DEADHEADING

After flowering, remove all the old flower heads with pruners. This stops the plant from putting all its energy into making seed, and maintains the neat rounded shape of the plant.

1 To keep your lavender plants young, bushy, and healthy, cut them back in late winter or early spring using clean, sharp hedge clippers.

2 Here you can see how the lavender has been cut just above where the new, green shoots meet the old, brown wood. This is very important as the old wood does not regenerate, which means that if you cut into it no new shoots will grow from the stems.

3 Shear the lavender as close as possible to the old wood without cutting into it. Work systematically along and around the hedge or each individual plant, keeping it as even as possible.

Stand back from time to time to check how evenly you are cutting

4 This form of pruning encourages the lavender to become very bushy, and to produce a greater volume of flowers. The plants then need to be deadheaded again as the flowers fade in summer.

PRUNING FOR
WINTER STEMS

Some dogwoods and willows are cut down almost to the ground each year, or every other year, to encourage masses of colorful young stems that provide a great winter display.

YOU WILL NEED

- pruners
- garden gloves
- garden compost
- slow-release fertilizer

SEE ALSO

- **PLANT A SHRUB** >> 110/111
- **CHOOSING SHRUBS** >> 140/143
- **PRUNING KNOW-HOW** >> 236/237

JARGON BUSTER

Fertilizers are a source of concentrated nutrients for plants.
Slow-release fertilizers do just that—they release nutrients slowly into the soil, because they degrade more slowly. They may be made of organic or inorganic material.

1 Remove weak, dead, or diseased growth to reduce congestion at the center. All winter-stem shrubs, like this dogwood, should be pruned in late winter or early spring.

Prune dead wood at the center of the plant for fuller regrowth the next year

Remove wispy stems to encourage the plant to sprout stronger shoots

Cut at a slight angle in the same direction as the bud

2 Cut back all the previous year's growth to the first pair of buds at the base of the stem. This will establish a system of young spurs, which will send out new stems.

3 Thin out some of the older, thicker spurs to reduce the chance of crossing stems that may rub and damage each other. Crossing growth will also make the plant look congested and untidy.

4 After pruning, you should be left with a simple, open structure from which a mass of strong, colorful new stems will grow. Add a layer of garden compost and a slow-release fertilizer around the base of the plant.

PLANTING
A **HEDGE**

The best time to plant a hedge is fall. Long-lived evergreens with dense foliage, such as yew, holly, or box, are ideal. Hawthorn, privet, and beech make good deciduous hedges. You can buy container-grown plants all year, and bare-root from late fall.

YOU WILL NEED

- spade
- well-rotted manure or compost
- string or twine
- wooden or card marker
- canes
- hedging plants, e.g., yew

SEE ALSO

- **PRUNING LAVENDER** >> 128/129
- **TRIM A HEDGE** >> 134/135

ADD MULCH

After planting, add a deep mulch of chipped bark or well-rotted manure, leaving gaps around the stems of the hedging plants. This will seal in moisture, deter weeds, and encourage rooting.

1 Dig over a strip, 3 ft (1 m) wide, to a spade's depth, and incorporate well-rotted manure or compost. Attach a line to mark the straight line of the hedge and dig a trench that's wide enough for the plants.

2 Make a planting guide by first marking a distance of 20–24in (50–60 cm) on a piece of wood or stiff card. Then place bamboo canes at these intervals along the string guide, and insert one plant beside each cane.

Use a cane to mark the planting position of each plant

3 Position plants at the same depth as they were originally; on bare-root types, look for the dark stain on the stem. Hold the plant firmly in place while you move the excavated soil back into the trench to support the roots.

4 Continue backfilling the trench and then firm the plants in with your foot, ensuring good contact between soil and roots. Don't press too hard. Roughly level the surface and water thoroughly.

TRIMMING
A **HEDGE**

Whether you have inherited a mature hedge or planted one that is thickening up well, you need to trim it regularly to maintain a dense barrier at the height you want. Hedges can also be clipped into interesting shapes and outlines as a garden feature.

YOU WILL NEED

- hedge clippers
- electric or gas hedge trimmer
- line of string (optional)
- protective gloves, goggles, and ear defenders

SEE ALSO

- **PLANT A HEDGE** >> 132/133
- **PRUNING LAVENDER** >> 128/129

EVERGREEN HEDGES

Many conifer hedges will not regrow if cut back into old wood. Yew is one of the few exceptions. It is important to trim them back at least twice a year, therefore; leave it too long and cutting back may result in bare patches.

TRIMMING A SMALLER HEDGE

1 Use hedge clippers to cut the top and sides of a small hedge. For a formal hedge you are aiming to achieve a flat surface, so use a line to keep your cutting straight if needed. For a less formal hedge you can cut to a more rounded shape.

TRIMMING A LARGER HEDGE

1 A mature hedge will put on considerable growth each year, and needs to be pruned in late summer to keep it to the desired size, cutting back to where the hedge was pruned the previous year. Use clippers for a small hedge or a power trimmer for a larger one.

Use safety goggles and ear defenders when operating a hedge trimmer

2 For a tall hedge, use a safety ladder to reach the top, cutting back to the previous summer's growth. Try to keep a straight edge as you work. Never over-stretch or lean out too far—get down and move the ladder instead.

MAKING A
TOPIARY CONE

Simple, architectural topiary shapes, such as
cones, are easy to create and suit many situations.
Allow a topiary plant to grow to the height you want
before trimming it to the desired shape.

YOU WILL NEED

- boxwood shrub
- long-handled clippers
- garden gloves (optional)

SEE ALSO

- **PLANT A SHRUB** >> 110/111
- **SHRUBS IN POTS** >> 112/115
- **PRUNING KNOW-HOW** >> 236/237

KEEP TOOLS CLEAN

To prevent the spread of
disease, sterilize your tools
before trimming a new
plant. Inexpensive household
disinfectant will do the job.
Rub on some oil after use,
to prevent rust.

Slightly
overgrown
plants with
recent growth
give you more
to work with

1 When buying
box or other topiary
plants, look for healthy
specimens densely
covered in unblemished
leaves, with a strong
leading upright shoot
in the center. Before
planting, ensure that
the plant's best side is
facing the front.

A topiary cone
adds structure
to the garden

Work slowly to avoid trimming too much off the plant initially

2 Stand above the plant, and locate a central shoot that will form the point at the top of the cone. With long-handled clippers, start to trim the box from this point in an outward direction. Keep moving around the plant as you clip.

3 Stand back from time to time to assess the shape of the cone. To achieve a perfectly circular cone, look directly down at it from the central point. From this position you can see if the cone is clipped equally all around.

4 If your cone has a few gaps, don't be tempted to keep trimming, or you will end up with a tiny topiary. Leave the gaps, and after a few months young shoots will form and fill them out. Tidy up your cone twice a year in summer.

REPOTTING
A SHRUB

All permanent shrubs need repotting into a bigger container, usually every two years in spring. This gives the roots more space to grow and an energizing "meal" of fresh soil.

YOU WILL NEED

- large container
- long kitchen knife
- hand fork
- pruners
- broken terra-cotta pieces
- multi-purpose potting soil
- watering can

SEE ALSO

- **SHRUBS IN POTS** >> 112/115
- **PRUNING LIGHTLY** >> 120/121
- **PRUNING SUMMER SHRUBS** >> 118/119

PLAN AHEAD

Shrubs, in general, prefer to remain undisturbed but they can be repotted, as shown here, when needed. Plan ahead by choosing a pot that will be large enough for the shrub to grow over the next two years.

1 Lay the pot on its side, ask someone to hold it, and gently ease out the plant by pulling its stem. If you're in danger of damaging the plant, or it is stuck, slide a long kitchen knife around the insides of the pot to free the root ball.

2 The roots will probably be in a tightly congested lump, in which case use a hand fork to prize out the encircling growth, and shake off the old "dead" soil and surface moss. Aim to create an open spread of roots.

Untangle gravel and other old debris from the roots

3 Cut back the main, thick, anchoring roots by up to one-third but leave the thin, fibrous roots unpruned. Pruning promotes the growth of more thin roots, which absorb moisture and nutrients.

4 Replace the old broken pots (for drainage) in the base of the new, bigger pot, pour in some potting soil, and position the plant. Once the plant is centered and upright, pour in more soil, firming it down, and water in well. Top off with gravel.

CHOOSING SHRUBS
FOR YEAR-ROUND INTEREST

Shrubs define the background of most gardens, providing color, structure, and texture throughout the year. Many can also form a central feature on account of their unusual foliage, flowers, or berries. Those chosen here provide interest over at least three seasons.

ABELIA
Abelia x grandiflora

A graceful flowering shrub with an attractive arching habit, abelia retains its glossy dark green leaves throughout winter, except in very cold areas. The pale pink, scented flowers appear in early summer and last until fall. It can reach 10 ft (3 m) in height and 12 ft (4 m) in spread. Plant in full sun in moist, well-drained soil.

MEXICAN ORANGE BLOSSOM
Choisya ternata 'Sundance'

This evergreen shrub has bright yellow foliage that can lighten a corner of any garden. The leaves are slightly darker in color when it is grown in the shade. In very cold areas, this plant requires a sheltered position, such as against a sunny wall. It grows up to 8 ft (2.5 m). Mexican orange blossom thrives in most well-draining soils.

DROOPING RED ENKIANTHUS
Enkianthus cernuus f. *rubens*
Preferring acidic or neutral soil, this is a medium to large, deciduous shrub that produces a colorful display of deep red, bell-shaped flowers that hang in clusters from late spring to summer. The leaves turn rich shades of red and purple in fall. This plant can reach 8 ft (2.5 m) and prefers a site with well-drained soil in sun or partial shade.

JAPANESE ARALIA
Fatsia japonica
The large, deeply lobed, evergreen leaves of this shrub inject color and texture into containers and borders, and the round clusters of tiny, white fall flowers and black fruits add to the effect. This plant is ideal for a city garden as it tolerates pollution. It can reach 10 ft (3 m), and will grow well in sun or partial shade in moist or well-drained soil.

PRICKLY HEATH
Gaultheria mucronata 'Wintertime'
Impressive, waxy white berries in fall and winter are the reason for growing this evergreen, spreading shrub. It produces small white flowers in late spring. Grow a male plant nearby to ensure a good crop of berries. It is relatively small at 4 ft (1.2 m) and likes moist, neutral to acid soil in sun or partial shade.

DOG HOBBLE
Leucothöe fontanesiana 'Scarletta'
Decorate a winter garden with this evergreen, mid- to back-of-border shrub, which has arching, red-tinged stems; green leaves; and cream, bell-shaped spring flowers. 'Scarletta' (above) has bronze-tinted winter leaves. Dog hobble is slow growing and reaches 5 ft (1.5 m) tall. It prefers shade or partial shade and a moist, acid soil.

PIERIS
Pieris formosa var. *forrestii* 'Wakehurst'
An evergreen shrub, pieris is grown for its attractive young spring foliage. The leaves of 'Wakehurst' are scarlet when young, changing to cream and then green. In spring it has clusters of white, bell-shaped flowers. Grow in sun or partial shade in a moist or well-drained, slightly acidic soil. It may reach 6 ft (2 m).

SKIMMIA
Skimmia japonica
This neat, evergreen shrub with dark green, glossy leaves has dense heads of tiny, fragrant, pink- or red-budded, white flowers in spring. If a male plant is nearby for pollination, female plants develop vivid red berries, which persist into winter. Skimmia thrives in a moist soil in partial shade and eventually grows to a height of 5 ft (1.5 m).

CHOOSING SHRUBS
FOR AUTUMN INTEREST

Shrubs can provide a welcome boost of color in the garden in fall, just when many other plants are starting to fade. Some of these tolerant and versatile plants have an astonishing and changing array of leaf colors from bright red to bronze and purple, and many have berries.

BLUEBEARD
Caryopteris x clandonensis 'Heavenly Blue'

This small shrub has beautiful blue flowers in late summer and early fall above decorative, aromatic, silvery-green foliage. 'Heavenly Blue' is popular for the intensity of its flower color. It is best planted in light, well-drained soil and grows to 3 ft (1 m). Keep it compact by cutting back to low buds in spring.

DOGWOOD
Cornus alba 'Sibirica'

In fall, the leaves of this dogwood turn rich shades of yellow, orange, and red before falling. It has bright red bare stems in winter, and bears flattened heads of white flowers in early summer, followed by bluish-white fruits. It can grow to about 10 ft (3 m) tall, and prefers a site in full sun in well-drained soil.

SMOKE BUSH
Cotinus 'Grace'
The broadly oval leaves of this shrub turn from purple to scarlet-red and flame-orange in fall. Whether purple- or green-leaved, all smoke bush varieties offer an eye-catching fall display, especially when backlit by the sun. 'Grace' grows to 20 ft (6 m) but can be pruned to keep it much smaller. It likes a well-drained, sunny site.

COTONEASTER
Cotoneaster horizontalis
A low-growing shrub, this is excellent for covering walls and fences, and is also suitable as ground cover. Cotoneaster plants produce bright red berries in the fall, which follow the small white summer flowers; both attract wildlife. Plant in full sun in well-drained soils. It reaches 3 ft (1 m), and can grow vigorously through other shrubs.

EUONYMUS
Euonymus alatus
A spreading, deciduous shrub, *Euonymus alatus* is valued mainly for its fall display, when the green foliage turns a spectacular crimson and scarlet, and purple and red fruits split open to reveal orange seed. It is ideal for the back of a mixed border, reaching about 6 ft (2 m), and likes sun or partial shade and moist soil.

OAK-LEAVED HYDRANGEA
Hydrangea quercifolia
The lobed leaves of this shrub make a fine backdrop for the cream, cone-shaped clusters flowers that develop from midsummer to fall. In fall, after developing maroon tints, the leaves take on striking red and purple hues. The plant reaches 6 ft (2 m) and likes moist soil and partial shade.

FIRETHORN
Pyracantha 'Mohave'
This evergreen shrub has prickly stems and produces clusters of white blooms in summer, followed by orange-red berries. Other varieties are also available, with fruits that ripen in shades of orange, red, and yellow. It prefers a sunny or slightly shady situation in well-drained soil, and can grow to 12 ft (4 m) .

ROSEHIP
Rosa 'Fru Dagmar Hastrup'
With its healthy crinkled foliage, this shrub rose produces single, fragrant, soft pink blooms in flushes from summer to early fall, and large, deep red, tomatolike hips alongside later flowers. The hips are attractive to birds. This plant reaches 3 ft (1 m) and prefers a well-drained soil in a sunny situation.

GRASSES

PLANTING GRASSES
IN THE GROUND

Most grasses are container-grown. The best times to plant them in the garden are in spring, to give them a whole growing season to settle in, or in fall, when the soil is warm and moist enough for the roots to grow strongly before winter.

YOU WILL NEED

- grasses grown in a container
- garden compost (optional)
- watering can or hose

SEE ALSO

- **CARING FOR GRASSES** >> 148/149
- **DIVIDING GRASSES** >> 154/155
- **CHOOSING GRASSES** >> 156/157

DECORATIVE GRASSES

Different grasses offer a wealth of colors, shapes, and sizes. Not all are green: grasses may be blue, red, bronze, or silver. Some provide fall color and others are evergreen. Choose to suit the style of your garden.

1 Dig a hole large enough to take the full depth of the container. Place the potted plant in the hole to ensure the top of the potting soil is level with the soil. Water the grass well in its pot before planting to give it a good start.

2 Remove the plant from its pot and gently tease out the roots around the edges of the root ball. This encourages them to grow out into the surrounding soil early.

3 Place the plant centrally into the hole, and fill in the dug out soil around the edges, firming gently with your fingers. Some people like to mix compost into the removed soil, but this is not absolutely necessary.

4 Using a watering can or hose, gently water in the plant. This not only provides it with moisture but ensures soil particles are washed into close contact with the roots. Keep the plant moist but don't over water.

CARING FOR
GRASSES

Ornamental grasses and grasslike plants are among the easiest to maintain of all garden plants, but low maintenance is not no maintenance: a little regular attention will keep them looking their best.

KEY POINTS

- **One of the attractions** of grasses is their ornamental seed heads. Only cut off the seed heads from grasses where self-seeding has become a problem. For example, grasses such as prairie dropseed or sedges could become problematic and self-seed.

- **Grasses that fade to brown** in fall and winter provide an interesting feature in the garden—one to enjoy as long as possible.

SEE ALSO

- **PLANTING GRASSES** >> 146/147
- **CUTTING GRASSES** >> 152/153
- **DIVIDING GRASSES** >> 154/155

JARGON BUSTER

Leaf rakes have thin metal prongs, in contrast to wider pronged plastic or bamboo rakes. They are ideal for removing leaf litter and mosses, or tidying other light garden materials, such as combing grasses.

Remember to spring clean Older leaves may go brown in winter. Affected leaves of small plants such as some sedges, acorus, luzula, and ophiopogon can be removed individually, but with larger plants such as festuca (above), it is quicker to comb the clump with a leaf rake.

Healthy and stressed grasses

Healthy grass leaves are usually flat and green right to the tips, indicating that the plant is growing well. A sign of stress is when leaves roll up into tubes. In dry conditions, this is a sign that the plant needs more water, because it is minimizing the surface area of its leaves to reduce moisture loss. In wet conditions, it can indicate the plant roots are too wet and the plant will need moving to a drier position.

Healthy blades of grass stand strong and upright

Healthy grass with flat, green leaves.

Stressed grass with leaves rolled into tubes.

Cut out dead or diseased foliage
Even grasses that stay green all year eventually fade and die off from the tips downward. Yellow or brown areas can be trimmed off with scissors, or the whole leaf cut off at its base.

Preventing excessive seedlings Some grasses and grasslike plants shed a lot of seed, and the resulting offspring can become problem weeds. To avoid this, simply cut off fading flowers before they start shedding seed, using pruners or scissors.

Grasses can add different textures and movement to the garden, providing an airy addition to a mixed border, or massed on their own, as here, for a modern, structural effect.

CUTTING BACK
GRASSES

It is important to cut back nonevergreen (deciduous) grasses hard to keep them looking their best. This can be done in late fall or, if you want to keep grasses uncut in winter for structure and interest, cut them back in early spring.

YOU WILL NEED

- pruners, or loppers, or electric hedge trimmer
- garden gloves

SEE ALSO

- **CARING FOR GRASSES** >> 148/149
- **DIVIDING GRASSES** >> 154/155
- **CHOOSING GRASSES** >> 156/157

JARGON BUSTER

Deciduous grasses are those that lose their green color and die back to a golden-brown shade in fall and winter. Like deciduous trees shedding old leaves in fall and winter to be replaced by new leaves in spring, deciduous grasses will start to show green shoots early in the year.

1 In late winter or early spring, cut back the previous summer's browned stems near ground level. If leaving to mid-spring to cut back early-flowering species, try not to damage any new green shoots.

Trim a few older stems at a time to avoid cutting back new growth

ALTERNATIVE METHODS

Thick stems or short leaves
Some grasses are too tough for garden clippers, and can injure bare skin. Protect your hands by wearing gloves or using long loppers for cutting.

Cutting back larger areas
It's quicker to use an electric hedge trimmer to cut back larger clumps. Cut the stems slightly higher than you would with clippers to avoid damaging new growth at the base.

2 Work your way methodically through the clump, removing all the old stems (which can be composted). Some grasses can be divided once cut back, while others are best divided when in active growth.

DIVIDING **GRASSES**

Most large grasses are easy to divide in fall or spring, giving you extra plants that may be particularly useful for spring plantings. Wait until late fall to late winter to divide *Stipa* grasses because they react badly to being divided earlier.

YOU WILL NEED

- saw or large serrated knife
- watering can

SEE ALSO

- **CARING FOR GRASSES** >> 148/149
- **CUTTING GRASSES** >> 152/153
- **CHOOSING GRASSES** >> 156/157

DON'T BURY THE CROWN

When planting in the ground, leave the crown of newly divided grasses slightly above the surface to discourage root rot, but do make sure the roots are covered or they will dry out.

Grasses can also be dug up after they've been cut back and then split

1 Remove the plant from the pot and look at its size and lines of growth to decide where best to divide it. This blue lyme grass (*Leymus arenarius*) lends itself to being split in two. Larger grasses may give three or four divisions.

2 Using a saw or large serrated knife, cut through the crown of the plant along the lines of least resistance. The crown is usually only a few centimeters deep, and cutting becomes easier once it is sliced.

Hold top and sides of plant to divide into two parts

3 Having cut through the crown, gently separate the rest of the root ball with your hands—this causes less damage to the fibrous grass root system than cutting it.

Both divisions should be a large size for replanting

4 Plant out the divided pieces in the same way as container plants, spacing them at least 12 in (30 cm) apart and watering them in well. Two or more clumps together are very effective in the garden bed.

CHOOSING GRASSES

A huge range of grasses is available to provide year-round interest in your garden, whether grown in containers, in mixed borders, or grouped as a feature. Relatively low maintenance, grasses offer a surprising variety of color and give a sense of movement to the garden.

FEATHER REED GRASS
Calamagrostis x acutiflora 'Karl Foerster'

A good choice in an informal border for a natural style of planting, 'Karl Foerster' is an upright grower with arrowlike flower heads reaching 5 ft (1.5 m). Its leaves and flowers withstand winter well, but need cutting back in spring before new growth starts. Grow in sun or partial shade, in moist, well-drained soil.

BOWLES' GOLDEN SEDGE
Carex elata 'Aurea'

One of the best known and most widely grown of all sedges, *C. elata* 'Aurea' is deciduous, shedding its leaves in fall. It forms an upright, arching fountain of golden-yellow leaves thinly edged in green, with small, blackish flower spikes in early summer. Preferring moist soils and part shade, it reaches a height of 30 in (75 cm).

PAMPAS GRASS
Cortaderia selloana 'Pumila'
A "dwarf" pampas grass, 'Pumila' grows up to 4 ft (1.4 m) in height. With plain green leaves, it is a very robust and reliable evergreen, featuring stout stems and abundant, long-lasting flower plumes. Less vigorous than some pampas varieties, it mixes well with other plants. It prefers a sunny site with moist or well-drained soil.

BLUE FESCUE
Festuca glauca
Fescues are small, narrow-leaved, clump-forming, largely evergreen grasses common in cool summer areas. Blue fescue's leaf color ranges from grayish-green to intense, silvery blue. Small flowers emerge blue and age to brown. It reaches a height of 12 in (30 cm) and prefers moist but well-drained soil in full sun or partial shade.

GOLDEN HAKONECHLOA
Hakonechloa macra 'Aureola'
An elegant, slow-growing grass from Japan, golden hakonechloa has narrow, arching, green-striped, bright yellow leaves, often reddish-tinged in fall and early winter. It looks magnificent in a tall container, which shows off its domed form. It grows to 10 in (25 cm) and prefers a moist but well-drained soil in full sun or partial shade.

JAPANESE BLOOD GRASS
Imperata cylindrica 'Rubra'
Japanese blood grass has upright leaves that emerge red-tipped, the red spreading down the leaf in summer, and peaking in fall. It reaches 18 in (45 cm), and in colder areas is best in a pot with winter protection. It likes a moist, well-drained soil in sun or partial shade. Can spread invasively and considered a pest in some areas of the US.

ZEBRA GRASS
Miscanthus sinensis 'Zebrinus'
This striking, horizontally banded grass forms arching mounds of foliage up to 8 ft (2.5 m) tall. The banding is temperature dependent, so the grass may be green in spring but stripes should appear by midsummer. It is deciduous, and old foliage needs to be removed in spring. It thrives in sunny conditions in a moist, well-drained soil.

BLACK MONDO GRASS
Ophiopogon planiscapus 'Nigrescens'
This is one of the few plants with truly black leaves. An evergreen that spreads slowly, it produces small, pale purple flowers in summer, then shiny, jet-black berries. It makes a modern edging to a border, and grows well in a pot. Reaching 6 in (15 cm), it likes full sun and part shade, and moist, well-drained soil.

SMALL
TREES

PLANTING
A **TREE**

Although planting a tree is a fairly simple task, a little attention to detail and the appropriate aftercare ensure a tree will fulfil its potential. Trees are long-lived and prominent within the garden, as well as expensive to buy, so it is worth planting them right.

YOU WILL NEED

- tree in a container, e.g., apple tree
- spade and fork
- cane stick
- stake and mallet
- tree tie
- well-rotted garden compost
- watering can with fine spray nozzle
- bucket
- pruners

SEE ALSO

- **MOVING TREES** >> 168/169
- **CHOOSING TREES** >> 170/171

JARGON BUSTER

A **root ball** is the mass formed by the network of roots and the soil that surrounds them. In a potted plant, the root ball is largely made up of potting soil, with the roots starting to show through.

1 Soak the root ball of the tree in its container before planting. This will compensate for any water loss from the roots during the planting process and ensure that the tree settles into its position well.

2 With a spade, dig a planting hole about three times as wide as the diameter of the pot and 12in (30cm) deep (most root activity takes place in the top layer of soil). Lightly fork the base and sides of the hole.

If soil on the sides of the hole is compacted, loosen it with a fork

Soaking the plant in a bucket of water before removing it from its pot also helps to loosen the roots from the root ball

Try not to break the roots as they are teased out

3 Check the hole is the correct depth by putting the pot in the hole and placing a cane across the top—it should rest on both sides of the hole and on the top of the root ball. You may need to add or remove soil in the hole.

4 Gently remove the root ball from its pot; the pot should slide off easily, leaving the root ball intact. Carefully tease out some of the larger encircling roots, to help the roots grow into the surrounding ground more successfully.

CONTINUED ▷

5 Stand the tree in the hole, viewing it from different angles. When you are happy with its position, drive a stout stake into the ground close to the tree trunk and at a 45-degree angle to avoid damaging the roots. Make sure that the stake faces into the prevailing wind.

6 Water in well as you backfill the soil around the hole. Unless the soil is poor or sandy, do not add organic matter because this seems to prevent the roots spreading out in search of nutrients. Firm the soil in gently.

Make a figure eight to hold the tree and the stake together

7 Tie the tree quite loosely to the stake with a tree tie, about 18 in (45 cm) from the ground, to allow the stem to flex in the wind. Check the tie regularly and loosen it as the tree girth expands, to prevent damage to the bark.

Water during dry spells during the first year or two

8 Water the tree well after planting and during dry periods for the first couple of seasons. Add a layer of well-rotted garden compost, about 3 in (8 cm) deep, around the tree. Keep the compost about 6 in (15 cm) away from the trunk.

9 Over the next two to three years, prune to form the shape of the tree. Use pruners to remove damaged wood or growth that spoils the tree's shape, such as crossing, rubbing branches. Cut fairly close to the main stem.

Magnolias come in a variety of forms, with bold and beautiful goblet- or star-shaped flowers. Many are compact and make a perfect feature plant for a smaller garden or for a large pot.

REMOVING
A **BRANCH**

If a branch is too large, too low, badly positioned, or diseased, it may need removing. Making careful, clean cuts will allow the tree to heal itself. Bad or rough cuts can allow disease to enter the wound, which can cause rotting, reducing the plant's potential lifespan.

YOU WILL NEED

- pruning saw
- garden gloves
- garden waste bag

SEE ALSO

- **PRUNE WINTER STEMS** >> 130/131
- **PRUNING KNOW-HOW** >> 236/237

WORK IN PAIRS

When cutting a heavy branch, ask someone to help support the weight when you saw. This can stop the branch from swinging or tearing and falling, and damaging the plant or injuring yourself.

1 Identify the branch that needs to be removed. Try to remove growth when it is young, as the recovery is faster. Trees and shrubs will recover better from several small wounds than one large one.

2 Make an undercut about 6in (15 cm) away from the trunk halfway through the branch. Make another cut from the top, slightly further away from the trunk. This will remove the main part of the branch without tearing.

Cutting at an angle helps water run off the cut, discouraging rot

3 Remove the remaining branch stub with a third cut, starting from the upper surface of the branch, just beyond the crease in the bark where the branch meets the trunk. Angle the cut away from the trunk. The cut surface will begin to shrink as the tree produces protective bark to cover it.

MOVING A
TREE OR SHRUB

Occasionally it is necessary to move a tree or shrub. It may have outgrown its position or you may simply want to take it with you when you move house. Unless the job is urgent, it's best to wait until the plant is dormant in fall or winter.

YOU WILL NEED

- spade and fork
- cane
- garden compost
- tarp or old blanket
- watering can
- pruners

SEE ALSO

- **PLANT A TREE** >> 160/163
- **REMOVE A BRANCH** >> 166/167

PREPARING TO MOVE

Moving can be stressful to trees and shrubs, so it is best done when they are dormant in fall and winter. Lightly prune to remove dead wood before the move, but do not prune hard.

1 Clear the ground around the plant to allow for easy access and digging. Choose a dry, mild day when the soil is workable, rather than attempting to dig into ground that is waterlogged or frozen.

Water the soil the day before so it is easy to work

2 Prepare the new hole in advance so the plant can be moved to its new position swiftly. Clear the area of weeds and make a circular hole large and deep enough to take the tree or shrub.

3 Carefully dig around the plant with a spade, trying to include as many of the fine roots as possible. As a rule of thumb, the roots should be as wide as the outer edge of the plant's canopy.

Small branches can be fragile so move the plant with care

5 Place the plant in the new hole and use a cane to check the planting depth. Make sure that the tree or shrub is planted no deeper than before, adding or taking away soil from the bottom of the hole as needed.

4 Lift the plant out of the hole and wrap the roots up in a tarp or old blanket. The idea is to prevent the roots from drying out, so transfer the plant to its new hole as soon as possible.

6 Water the plant in well and continue to water for the following spring and summer. Apply a layer of mulch to retain moisture. If any branches die back after the move, prune them back to healthy wood. Keep the site free of weeds.

CHOOSING TREES
FOR SMALL GARDENS

This selection includes some of the most reliable and popular small trees. Many are chosen for their ornamental features, from the elegant flowers of the star magnolia to the fireworklike leaves of the Japanese maple. This guide will help you choose the right tree for the right spot.

JAPANESE MAPLE
Acer palmatum **'Sango-kaku'**

Japanese maples are small trees or large shrubs with intricate or pretty leaves, and often fine fall color. 'Sango-kaku' (also called 'Senkaki') is known as the coral bark maple due to its orange-red branches and trunk, a beautiful winter feature. Its leaves open pinkish-yellow, becoming green in summer and yellow in fall. It reaches 20 ft (6 m).

REDBUD
Cercis canadensis **'Forest Pansy'**

This striking, multi-stemmed tree has heart-shaped, deep red-purple foliage that turns to orange and bronze in fall. Reaching up to 26 ft (8 m), 'Forest Pansy' bears clusters of small, pink flowers in spring before the leaves appear. It prefers fertile, moisture-retentive, well-drained soil in a sunny or partially shady position.

CORNELIAN CHERRY
Cornus mas

A small, spreading tree or shrub, Cornelian cherry has green oval leaves that turn purple in autumn. It produces clusters of tiny, bright yellow flowers in winter, followed by red, cherrylike fruit. Growing up to 13 ft (4 m), this tree is best planted in well-drained soil in sun or partial shade at the back of a border or as part of an informal hedge.

STAR MAGNOLIA
Magnolia stellata

This small tree, which grows up to 10 ft (3 m) tall, produces beautiful white, star-shaped flowers, which emerge before the dark-green, narrow, oval leaves, and can be vulnerable to spring frost. 'Rosea' has flowers with a rosy pink center. It tolerates most soils that are moist but well drained, and prefers a sunny or partially shady spot.

CRAB APPLE
Malus 'John Downie'

A vigorous, ornamental crab apple tree, 'John Downie' produces an abundance of bright red to orange-yellow crab apples in fall. Reaching up to 30 ft (10 m), it has showy white spring blossoms that are ideal for pollinating other apple trees nearby. Plant in a sunny position, although it tolerates partial shade, and in moderately fertile, well-drained soil.

CHINESE TUPELO
Nyssa sinensis

A tree or large shrub that reaches 26–39 ft (8–12 m), the Chinese tupelo has deciduous leaves that display a wide array of fall colors from mellow yellows to fiery oranges and reds. The green-gray bark takes on an interesting flaky texture as it matures. Plant in full sun or partial shade, in fertile, well-drained, acidic soil.

KILMARNOCK WILLOW
Salix caprea 'Kilmarnock'

Forming a distinctive mushroom shape, this small willow has long, trailing branches. In late winter, silver-colored "pussy willow" catkins appear. Thin out select stems and prune away dead wood to keep the head airy and maintain the shape of the tree. It can grow to about 6 ft (2 m) in height and spread and prefers well-drained soil in a sunny spot.

WHITE CEDAR
Thuja occidentalis 'Rheingold'

This slow-growing evergreen conifer reaches up to 3–5 ft (1–1.5 m). Its bushy, bronze-tinged, amber-yellow foliage makes a lovely centerpiece in beds and borders. 'Rheingold' prefers moist, well-drained soil in full sun. The foliage becomes richer in color in winter, but may need some protection from damaging, drying winds.

VEGETABLES

GROWING
SEEDS IN TRAYS

Growing crops from seed is simple and economical, and sowing in flats is a good idea as they are easy to clean and reuse, and fit perfectly into propagators or on bright windowsills.

YOU WILL NEED

- vegetable seeds, e.g., lettuce, radish, spinach, or other salad vegetables
- detergent or sterilizing solution
- seed flats
- cell trays
- seed or multi-purpose potting soil
- propagator
- watering can with fine spray nozzle

SEE ALSO

- **SOWING SEEDS OUTDOORS** >> 24/25
- **SEEDS IN POTS** >> 178/179
- **GROWING PLUG PLANTS** >> 180/181

JARGON BUSTER

Damping off is a fungal disease that affects seedlings, particularly those grown under cover. The fungus attacks stems, causing them to collapse and die. This is why it is vital to wash and sterilize flats if you are reusing them.

1 Fill a flat with multi-purpose or seed potting mix, and use a second tray to gently firm it to remove air pockets. You can clean and recycle food packaging to use as seed trays, with holes pierced in the bottom.

2 Scatter seeds evenly over the soil, either straight from the packet or sprinkling them from the palm of your hand. Sow thinly to prevent waste and overcrowding, which can result in spindly seedlings that are more prone to disease.

Humidity can encourage disease, so remove the lid once the seedlings have emerged

3 After lightly covering seeds with sifted soil, water gently with a sprinkling of tap water to avoid disturbing the seeds; avoid using stored rainwater, which can cause damping off disease. Label the tray with the plant name and date.

4 Place the flat in a propagator or cover it with clear plastic to create the warmth and humidity needed for germination. Keep in a light place, such as on a windowsill, but not in strong sun. Remove the cover as soon as seedlings emerge.

CONTINUED ▷

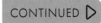

5 When the seedlings have a few leaves, transplant them into cell trays or small pots. To do this, water the seedlings, then hold a seed leaf and loosen the roots with a dibble or pencil to gently tease each one from the soil.

6 Have ready cell trays or small pots filled with multi-purpose potting soil, then water and allow them to drain. Make a hole using a dibble in each cell, insert a seedling, and then gently firm. Water in and label.

7 After a few weeks, harden off the seedlings by gradually exposing them to the outdoor environment. Set them outside during the day and bring them in at night, or place them in a cold frame and gradually increase the ventilation.

A cold frame or greenhouse is best for seedlings to ensure that they also get enough light

SOWING SEEDS
IN SMALL POTS

Make use of small pots to grow larger vegetable seeds. These single seedlings will grow on under cover with minimal disturbance before planting in the ground or a large container outdoors.

YOU WILL NEED

- larger seeds of your choice
- small pots
- multi-purpose potting soil
- plant labels
- propagator, or clear plastic and elastic bands or string
- watering can with fine spray nozzle

SEE ALSO

- **GROWING TOMATOES** >> 184/185
- **GROW CLIMBING BEANS** >> 186/187
- **GROW ROOT VEGETABLES** >> 190/191

WATERING POTS

Water small pots by placing them in a tray of water until the soil surface feels damp, then remove and allow to drain. This helps to prevent seeds and seedlings from being disturbed.

1 Sowing in small pots works well for larger seeds and where fewer plants are required. Fill the pots with multi-purpose potting soil, firm gently, and push the seed in to the correct planting depth. Label and water.

2 Cover pots with clear plastic, or put in a propagator until the seeds germinate. Keep pots moist and turn them on sunny windowsills daily to stop plants growing toward the light and ensure that they grow straighter.

Potbound plants, as shown here, may need roots teased out before planting outdoors

3 Get plants gradually accustomed to being outdoors by placing them outside in the day and bringing them in at night. Plant them out into large pots or the ground before the roots become restricted, and water in well.

GROWING VEGETABLES
FROM PLUG PLANTS

If space and time for growing vegetables from seed are tight, buy plug plants at garden centers or by mail order. These are seedlings with a small root system, ready to plant out. They are more expensive than seed and the choice of varieties is limited, but they do offer an easy way to get started.

YOU WILL NEED

- plug plants, e.g., squash
- shredded bark
- plant labels
- support sticks or canes
- cloches (optional)
- watering can

SEE ALSO

- **GROWING TOMATOES** >> 184/185
- **GROWING POTATOES** >> 192/193

JARGON BUSTER

Cloches are large, transparent, bell-shaped structures that can be placed over individual plants to protect against cold and windy weather. They are also useful to ward off slugs, snails, and other pests.

Once made of glass, cloches are now available in plastic, and are lightweight and portable.

1 Buy compact, green plants with a healthy root system. Water well and plant out or pot on immediately to avoid checking their growth. Beware of buying squash and other tender plants before the risk of frost has passed.

Plug plants are vulnerable once removed from packaging so be ready to plant immediately

3 Gently firm the soil around each plant so that it is stable, and water well to help it get established. Add a mulch of organic material around each plant (but not touching the stem) to retain soil moisture and prevent weeds.

2 Carefully remove each seedling from its packaging and, holding the root ball rather than the delicate leaves, plant it into prepared soil so that the top of the root ball is just below soil level.

4 Label, and add supports for plants that need them as they grow. Cloches are often useful to protect young plants from cold and windy weather. Continue to water the plants regularly until they are established.

RAISING LETTUCES
ON A WINDOWSILL

For fresh salad leaves on hand whenever you need them, sow cut-and-come-again lettuces on a kitchen windowsill. Loose-leaf lettuces can be sown thickly, the baby leaves cut, and stumps allowed to regrow.

YOU WILL NEED

- loose-leaf lettuce seeds
- multi-purpose potting soil
- long, slim pots or fabric bags
- woven willow surrounds
- pencil or dibble
- watering can with fine spray nozzle

SEE ALSO

- **GROWING PLUG PLANTS** >> 180/181
- **GROW CLIMBING BEANS** >> 186/187
- **GROW ROOT VEGETABLES** >> 190/191

LETTUCES THAT NEED MORE SPACE

Butterhead, romaine, and crisphead lettuces develop dense central hearts of leaves. Sow seed in trays and plant out seedlings 8–12 in (20–30 cm) apart.

1 Long, slim pots or fabric bags fit snugly onto a windowsill and look attractive with woven willow surrounds. Fill them with potting soil to about 1/2 in (1 cm) below the rim and make drills 1/4 in (1/2 cm) deep and 2 in (5 cm) apart.

2 Pour seed into the palm of your hand and sprinkle it into each drill using your thumb and forefinger. Cover seeds lightly with potting soil and water using a can with a fine spray nozzle to avoid disturbing the seeds.

3 Keep the potting soil moist and when the seedlings are 2–4 in (5–10 cm) in height, cut them as required, about 1 in (2.5 cm) above soil level. The plants should then sprout new leaves, which can be harvested about two weeks later.

Lettuces can be cut to the stump to regrow two or three times

GROWING
TOMATOES

Home-grown tomatoes taste divine straight from the vine, and make beautiful displays when dripping with fruit. Sow seed indoors in early spring and pot on as plants grow, or buy young plants in late spring.

YOU WILL NEED

- tomato plants, such as the indeterminate varieties shown here
- large pot
- multi-purpose potting soil
- canes
- garden twine
- liquid tomato fertilizer
- watering can

SEE ALSO

- **WINDOWSILL LETTUCES** >> 182/183
- **GROW CLIMBING BEANS** >> 186/187

JARGON BUSTER

Indeterminate varieties are tall and need staking, while **determinate varieties** are a bit more compact.

Cherry tomatoes will ripen earlier, while larger types like **beefsteaks** ripen later in the season.

1 Once nights are frost free and plants are acclimated to being outdoors, fill a pot, at least 10 in (25 cm) wide, with compost to 2 in (5 cm) below the rim. Plant the tomato deeply, as the section of buried stem will send out extra roots.

2 Tall indeterminate cultivars need training up a support. Push a couple of long bamboo canes or other stakes into the potting soil and tie in the main stem to keep the plant stable. Bush and trailing types do not need supports.

Make sure the pot is cleaned before using to plant your tomatoes

3 As the plant grows, tie the main stems loosely to the canes. Pinch out fast-growing suckers growing between the leaves and main stem on indeterminate cultivars. Leave side shoots to develop on determinate types.

Suckering also helps to stimulate new growth

4 Water regularly. When the first fruits appear, feed weekly with a tomato fertilizer, and add extra potting soil if the roots become exposed. Pinch out the growing tip as the plant reaches the top of its cane. Ripe fruits twist off easily.

GROWING
CLIMBING BEANS

Climbing French beans and runner beans grow best in a rich, fertile soil, so prepare your site by digging in plenty of well-rotted organic matter at least two weeks before planting. Grow companion plants nearby, such as nasturtiums, to attract pollinating insects to the garden.

YOU WILL NEED

- bean seeds, e.g., runner beans, climbing French beans
- nasturtium plants
- 8 bamboo canes 7 ft (2.2 m) long
- garden twine
- watering can

SEE ALSO

- **GROWING TOMATOES** >> 184/185
- **GROW ROOT VEGETABLES** >> 190/191
- **GROWING POTATOES** >> 192/193

JARGON BUSTER

Companion planting in vegetable gardening is when different types of plants are grown nearby to benefit each other or a particular crop.

For example, scented nasturtiums are used here to attract pollinating insects for the benefit of both the nasturtiums and the climbing beans.

1 Support is vital for these climbing plants. Build a wigwam from eight canes, ideally at least 7 ft (2.2 m) long, pushed firmly into the soil about 12 in (30 cm) apart, in a circle. Tie the canes securely at the top and again halfway down.

Runner beans are best sown from mid-May to July

2 From late spring, when the soil is at least 54°F (12°C), plant two seeds at a depth of 2in (5cm) by each cane and water thoroughly. In cold areas or where the soil is heavy, sow the seeds in deep pots indoors in mid-spring.

3 After germination, remove the weaker seedling. Twist the remaining plant around its cane and tie it in with twine. A companion nasturtium plant will attract pollinating insects to the runner bean flowers, promoting a good crop.

4 It is important to pick beans regularly (at least twice a week), when they are young and tender, because over-mature pods are less appetizing and suppress the formation of new flowers.

Tomatoes taste so much better when picked fresh from your own garden for summer salads and sandwiches. They are cheap, easy to cultivate, and can be grown in containers in a small garden or even on a balcony.

GROWING
ROOT CROPS

Easy to grow and wonderfully sweet when scrubbed and eaten fresh, most root crops thrive when sown outdoors, the seedlings thinned, and crops watered regularly. If you are sowing them in containers, choose deep pots with room for the roots to develop.

GROWING RADISHES

Summer radishes An ideal crop for beginners, radishes are undemanding, fast growing, and delicious when freshly picked. Sow outdoors from early spring until late fall. Scatter seeds thinly or sow in rows 2 in (5 cm) apart at a depth of about ½ in (1 cm). When the seedlings appear, thin radishes promptly to make space for rapid growth: space radishes 1 in (2 cm) apart and keep pots well watered.

YOU WILL NEED

- vegetable seeds, e.g., carrots and radishes, shown here
- large, deep containers, e.g., pots or growing bags
- multi-purpose potting soil
- scissors
- frost blanket
- sticks or chopsticks

SEE ALSO

- **SOWING SEEDS OUTDOORS** >> 24/25
- **WINDOWSILL LETTUCES** >> 182/183

WINTER RADISHES
Larger winter cultivars of radishes are slower to mature, and should be sown from mid- to late summer. Winter roots, such as 'Mantanghong,' can take several months until they are ready to harvest.

GROWING CARROTS

1 Large, deep containers, such as these bags, are ideal for growing carrots. Ensure that the soil surface is level and make a shallow drill about ½in (1 cm) deep, sow seeds thinly along it, cover with potting soil, and water well.

2 When the seedlings have their first divided leaves, thin them to about 2in (5 cm) apart, either by pulling them up between your fingers or by snipping off the plants with scissors at soil level. Remove and compost all thinnings.

3 Carrot flies fly close to the ground and can be prevented from reaching your crops by creating a barrier with a frost blanket that, with the pot, is 24in (60 cm) high, or by raising the container the same height off the ground.

GROWING
EARLY POTATOES

Potatoes are easy to grow and usually ready to harvest after they have flowered. At 10–12 weeks, pull some soil aside to check whether the tubers are ready, and lift the roots carefully with a fork.

YOU WILL NEED

- sprouted ("chitted") seed potatoes
- egg crates
- garden string
- sticks for markers
- spade
- rake
- general-purpose fertilizer

SEE ALSO

- **POTATOES IN A TRASH CAN** >> 194/195
- **DEAL WITH PESTS** >> 244/245

SEED POTATOES

Available from late winter, seed potatoes look like ordinary potatoes but are certified free of viruses. Buy them from a local garden center or supplier. All potatoes grow better after "chitting," shown in step 1.

1 In late winter, place your seed potatoes in egg crates or trays with the maximum number of buds (eyes) pointing upward. Stand the crates in a cool, light place indoors for about six weeks to produce sturdy, dark sprouts (chitting).

3 Fill each hole with soil, rake over the row, and mark its position. A general-purpose fertilizer can also be applied at the specified rate on either side of the row at this stage, or it may be worked into the soil before planting.

2 When shoots reach about 1 in (2.5 cm) long, in early spring, mark a row on prepared soil. At 12 in (30 cm) intervals dig holes about 4 in (10 cm) deep and plant a single tuber in each, with its shoots pointing upward.

4 Tubers exposed to light will turn green, making them toxic and inedible. To avoid this, hill up the plants as they emerge by mounding soil around their stems to a height of around 6 in (15 cm).

GROWING **POTATOES** IN A TRASH CAN

Potatoes taste best when freshly harvested. Grow them in deep trash cans, and plant "earlies," "second earlies," and "maincrops" for tubers in separate trash cans so you can harvest crops over a long period.

YOU WILL NEED

- sprouted ("chitted") potatoes
- egg crates
- large trash can
- multi-purpose potting soil
- watering can

SEE ALSO

WATER REGULARLY

The large, leafy potato plants and developing tubers need a reliable supply of water to produce a good harvest. Keep potting soil moist but not wet, and make sure trash cans have holes in the bottom for drainage.

1 Sprout ("chit") potatoes before planting. In early spring, place seed potatoes in egg crates, with the end with the most eyes facing upward, and set them on a cool windowsill. Plant when the shoots are 3/4in (2 cm) long.

2 From mid- to late spring, make drainage holes in the base of the trash can and fill one third with potting soil. Evenly space five potatoes or fewer on the surface, shoots pointing up. Cover with 6 in (15 cm) of soil and water well.

Even three seed potatoes, if using a smaller trash can, will produce a good crop

3 Add potting soil around the plants in stages as they grow until the trash can is full. Known as "hilling up," this encourages more tubers to form, prevents them turning green and poisonous on exposure to light, and reduces frost damage.

4 With consistent watering, potatoes should be ready to crop when the plants flower. Empty the trash can and harvest the tubers all at once or allow plants to continue growing and pick through the soil to take what you need.

HERBS

GROWING
HERBS FROM SEED

Garden catalogs list thousands of different seeds and make for stimulating reading—especially over the winter. Many seeds are easy to grow, and starting from seed is an inexpensive way to expand your collection of both basic and unusual herbs.

YOU WILL NEED

- packets of seeds of your choice, e.g., basil, chervil, coriander, dill, lemon verbena, and parsley
- selection of small-sized pots and module trays
- seed or starting soil
- vermiculite
- watering can with fine spray nozzle

SEE ALSO

- **AN HERB GARDEN** >> 204/205
- **GROW HERB CUTTINGS** >> 210/213
- **DIVIDING HERBS** >> 214/215

JARGON BUSTER

Vermiculite is a naturally occurring mineral that helps to retain moisture and nutrients in the soil.

It also provides insulation for seeds as they grow and develop.

LARGER SEEDS

1 Seeds of this size are the easiest to handle. Check the instructions, make sure your palm is dry, and gently scatter at the correct spacing. Use just enough and return the rest to the packet.

2 Planting depth and light requirements vary for each type of herb. Follow the packet's instructions and scatter an appropriate depth of vermiculite over the seeds.

3 Use a waterproof pen to label the pot. It is useful to record the date of sowing so you can check for signs of growth at the supplier's suggested times.

DIPPING HOLES

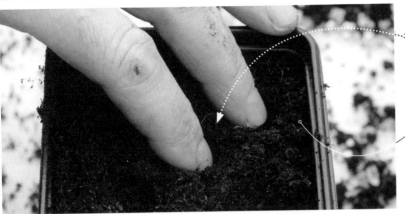

1 For seeds that need to be accurately spaced and at a greater depth, use your fingertips to make indentations in the soil at a suitable depth and distance apart.

When pressing down on soil, also check moisture levels

2 With big seeds, place one or two in each hole, but with smaller seeds, put in a few more each time. Try not to drop them from high up as they can bounce and be easily lost.

3 Cover with a 50:50 vermiculite and fine potting soil mix. Gently firm, label, and water carefully. Place in a warm, light place. Keep barely moist and check regularly for signs of growth.

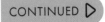

CONTINUED ▷

FINE SEEDS

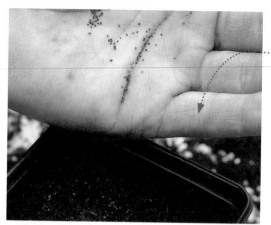

1 Lightly dust the seed from your palm or "pinch" a small amount between finger and thumb and carefully sprinkle it. Don't sow more seeds in a single pot than advised on the packet instructions.

2 Finer seeds need a lighter covering of vermiculite using a finer grade, and some need to be left exposed. Avoid over watering as too much can flush seeds into one corner.

3 Remember to water your seedlings and continue growing them in a bright, airy place. If the right numbers of seeds are sown in the right container, no pricking out will be needed, just potting up later on.

SOWING PLUGS

1 Cell trays come in sizes from four large plugs to many hundreds of small ½in (1 cm) squares, and are ideal for sowing seeds where you only need one or two plants to grow in each cell. It is usually best to avoid sowing thickly. Dense sowing results in seedlings that are weak and more susceptible to disease.

2 So you don't lose track of where you are, sow larger seeds on the surface of all the cells and then press them down to the correct depth before covering in one go.

Fine potting soil is easy for seeds to push through

3 Pinch out excess seedlings, leaving the strongest with plenty of space to grow on. Pot up into a larger container or plant out when the plug is well filled with roots.

Culinary seedlings that are pinched out can be used up in cooking in the kitchen

Herbs such as tarragon, rosemary, sage, and bay are easy to grow and suit town and country gardens. Many can provide fragrance all year round, and color from spring to late summer.

PLANTING
AN **HERB GARDEN**

This formal herb feature takes only a day to build and a season to mature. Here, bricks have been used to edge the beds and divide them into quarters. A potted bay tree forms the centerpiece.

YOU WILL NEED

- pot-grown herbs, e.g., bay tree, camomile, chives, rosemary, sage, thyme
- garden stakes and string
- bricks
- hammer
- garden compost
- watering can

SEE ALSO

- **HERBS FROM SEED** >> 198/201
- **GROW HERB CUTTINGS** >> 210/213
- **DIVIDING HERBS** >> 214/215

COMMON HERBS

Commonly grown culinary herbs include basil, chervil, cilantro, dill, marjoram, oregano, parsley, sage, and arugula. Some herbs, such as mint, can quickly take over an herb garden so are best confined in pots.

1 Mark out a cross with stakes and string. Dig trenches following the string lines, slightly wider and not quite as deep as the bricks to allow space for the bricks to settle. Use a hammer handle to firm in the bricks.

2 Finish the last quarter and bed the bricks down securely, packing the soil firmly against them (no need to mortar them in). If you wish to have a plant in the center of the feature, make sure that you leave space for it.

This is a handy way to use up old or spare bricks in an herb garden

Bay needs regular clipping as it can get very big and quickly outgrow its space

3 Arrange the plants in their pots before they go in the ground, so you can adjust the spacing if required. Water each plant thoroughly before removing it from its pot. Make planting holes and insert the plants. Water in well.

4 Finish off the design with a central plant—a bay tree, which can be clipped into shape, has been used here. Water all the plants regularly until they are fully established, especially in hot, dry weather.

PLANTING AN HERB
HANGING BASKET

Edible and aromatic herbs can look spectacular in a hanging basket that is planted with a range of leaf colors and textures. Hang it near the kitchen or grill for tempting smells and a readily accessible herb garden.

YOU WILL NEED

- herbs, e.g., basil, silver thyme, chives
- hanging basket, hook, and liner
- potting soil
- small hand trowel
- skewers
- watering can

SEE ALSO

- **AN HERB GARDEN** >> 204/205
- **GROW HERB CUTTINGS** >> 210/213

🌿 HERB NEIGHBORS

With limited space, choose herbs for your hanging basket that you are most likely to use or enjoy for their taste or aroma. For example, try tarragon, chives, and oregano. Avoid large, woody herbs such as bay and rosemary.

1 Check that the basket has a good number of drainage holes in the base and sides—a skewer pushed through the liner several times from the outside will help. Partially fill with top-quality fresh potting soil and gently firm.

3 Add more fresh potting soil
around the roots, gently firming
down in stages, until the herbs are
at the same planting level as in their
pots. Trim back any damaged stems
or bruised leaves and use in cooking.

Silver-
leaved
foliage
adds
contrast

Break up soil
with your hands
if it is lumpy

2 Carefully remove the plants from
their pots and if the roots are
congested, gently tease them out
a little. Arrange and space out the
hardy herbs first, filling larger gaps
with tender herbs such as basil.

4 Water your basket well before
hanging it, and check that excess
moisture drains away. Choose a sunny
spot. Select a robust hook and hang
carefully as large baskets can be very
heavy, especially when wet.

MAKING
A **LAVENDER HEDGE**

Attractive to look at and much loved by bees and butterflies, this aromatic feature is easy to grow, requiring no feeding and little maintenance beyond an annual clip as the flowers begin to fade.

YOU WILL NEED

- lavender plants, e.g., 'Hidcote' or 'Munstead' varieties
- spade
- small garden trowel
- coarse sand
- gravel
- watering can

SEE ALSO

- **AN HERB GARDEN** >> 204/205
- **PRUNING LAVENDER** >> 128/129

PRESS IN
YOUNG PLANTS

Young plants need to be firmly planted. Do this by gently pressing soil in toward the roots themselves rather than pressing downward on the root ball.

Lavenders can cope with poor soil and like good drainage

1 Thoroughly dig over the ground, removing large stones and all traces of stubborn weeds. Add coarse sand to heavy soil, but do not add any fertilizer or bulky organic matter unless your soil is very sandy.

A site in full sun is best for planting a lavender hedge

Tease out the roots slightly at the base of the root ball

2 Dig holes a little larger than the plant pots and, when using larger lavenders such as 'Hidcote' or 'Munstead,' space your plants about 12–16in (30–40 cm) apart. Space smaller varieties 10in (25 cm) apart.

3 Firm in your plants so the soil is at the same level as the potting soil. On heavy or wet soil, place the plants ³⁄₄in (2 cm) above the surrounding soil and add a layer of gravel sufficient to just cover the plant's root ball.

4 Water in well immediately after planting and keep moist over their first summer or until established, but don't over water lavender. Avoid pouring water over the top of the plant, and direct it instead to the surrounding soil at the base.

GROWING HERBS
FROM CUTTINGS

Many plants do not produce viable seed or, if they do, it is so fussy or slow to grow that it is easier and quicker to take cuttings from your favorite plant. Always keep your new cuttings moist and in a warm, sunny place.

SOFTWOOD CUTTINGS

YOU WILL NEED

- cuttings from plants, e.g., rosemary, camomile, thyme, mint
- small plant pots and cell trays
- small pruners or scissors
- fine potting soil
- vermiculite
- watering can with fine spray nozzle

SEE ALSO

JARGON BUSTER

Softwood cuttings are the soft and pliable young shoots of a plant or shrub.

Woodier cuttings are taken from slightly thicker, woody stems.

Aerial roots are roots that form above the ground.

Water sprouts are new shoots that spring up directly from the roots.

1 In late summer, select a nonflowering shoot 3–4 in (7.5–10 cm) long from a healthy-looking plant. Try to avoid any stems that are too young and soft as these are more difficult to root.

2 Cut just below a leaf node using clean, sharp pruners and remove the leaves from the bottom half of the cutting. Prepare one cutting at a time so it does not dry out and deteriorate.

Use your fingertips to feel for the knobby leaf node that holds leaves on a plant

3 Insert the cutting 1¼–1¾in (3–4 cm) deep into a 50:50 vermiculite and fine soil mix. If the cutting bends too easily, it is too young or the soil is too coarse. Water well.

Clear any debris from the potting soil, such as small twiggy strands

CONTINUED ▷

WOODIER CUTTINGS

1 Select a firm, slightly woody, nonflowering side shoot 2–4in (5–10 cm) long and gently cut or pull it away from the main stem so a sliver of bark remains on the cutting.

2 Trim any wispy strands from the heel and carefully remove all the leaves from the lower half. Insert the cutting into a 50:50 vermiculite and fine soil mix. Water well.

LAZY CUTTINGS

Look carefully at the underside of herbs such as camomile and thyme and you will see aerial roots growing from their stems. These stems will develop happily if detached and grown on in their own plug or pot.

ROOT CUTTINGS

 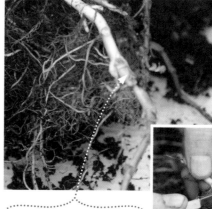 

1 For herbs with invasive roots, such as mint, divide the parent plant into good-sized portions with large fleshy roots for potting up individually. Do not reuse the old potting soil.

2 Select a long, healthy, firm root with a diameter of at least 1/4in (5mm). Look for knobby structures (nodes), which appear at intervals and may already be sprouting new roots and shoots.

3 Cut a section 2–2³/₄in (5–7 cm) long, with at least one node. Insert vertically into your potting mix. Consider growing more than is needed to insure against loss.

PROPAGATING MINT SUCKERS

1 Remove water sprouts from container plants—they root if they touch bare soil. Keep one or two for cuttings, but dispose of the rest carefully; they grow well on the compost heap.

2 Cut just above a leaf node into segments 2¾–4 in (7–10 cm) long and insert four or five into each small pot, so at least one pair of small young leaves is above the surface.

PINCHING OUT

Pinch out parts that are leaning over or looking untidy to leave behind the strongest growth

Sometimes there may not be adequate cutting material available. New side shoots will grow quickly if the top 2–4 in (5–10 cm) are pinched out. These shoots might make good cuttings.

DIVIDING **HERBS**

Many small-leaved, spreading, or mat-forming herbs can be easily multiplied by dividing and growing on more from a single plant. This is best done in late spring or early summer when the parent plant is in active growth.

DIVISION BY CUTTING UP

1 Using sharp scissors, trim excess leafy growth from around the sides and lightly trim the top. This is most easily done with the plant still in its pot. Compost the trimmings.

2 Carefully remove the pot (for washing and reuse) and slice or cut the root ball in half. The bottom part can be discarded and composted as it is likely to be exhausted and filled with roots.

YOU WILL NEED

- small and large plant pots
- plant labels
- scissors or sharp knife
- fine potting soil, well-draining potting soil, and vermiculite
- watering can

SEE ALSO

- **HERBS FROM SEED** >> 198/201
- **AN HERB GARDEN** >> 204/205
- **GROW HERB CUTTINGS** >> 210/213

JARGON BUSTER

Leggy plants have a spindly and untidy appearance. They tend to flop over and produce fewer flowers.

Plants can become leggy for a number of reasons, such as not enough sunlight or nutrients in the soil.

3 With this herb, the aim is to make plugs with a surface area of about ³/₄x³/₄in (2x2 cm). By carefully cutting using scissors or a sharp knife it is possible to generate nine or ten good plugs.

4 Fill each pot with fine soil, firm down, and make a hole with your finger about ³/₄in (2 cm) deep. Insert one plug in each hole, gently firm in place, and water well.

5 Label each pot with the plant name and the propagation date. Place in a bright, warm spot and keep moist. Results should be clearly visible within a couple of weeks.

RESUSCITATING LEGGY PLANTS

Remember to tease out the roots slightly

Leggy plants can be rescued to provide new plants or one compact large one. Partially fill a larger pot with potting soil and insert the herb. Cover the woody stems with soil up to the base of the leaves. Firm and keep moist until new roots develop, then divide the plant or use its stems for cuttings.

TEASING APART

Many pots of congested seedlings, such as basil, parsley, and chives, can be divided. The stems and roots are very fragile, so prize apart the clumps into no more than half a dozen portions.

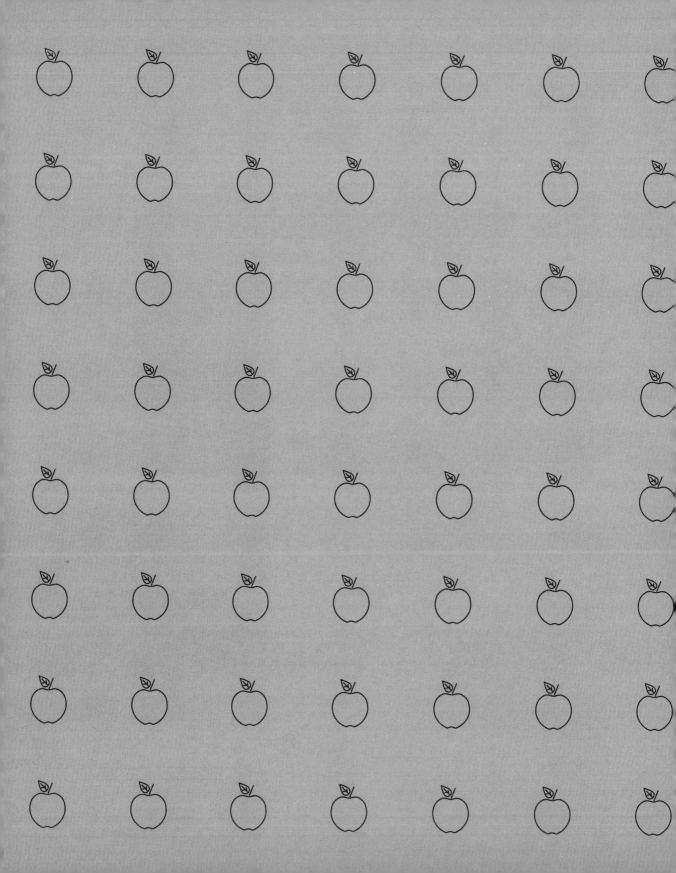

FRUIT

PLANTING A BASKET
OF STRAWBERRIES

Hanging baskets are a great way to make extra space for crops in small gardens, and look particularly beautiful when in flower or overflowing with ripe strawberries.

YOU WILL NEED

- strawberry plants
- hanging basket with bracket
- large plant pot
- plastic liner
- scissors
- multi-purpose potting soil
- water-retaining crystals (optional)
- liquid tomato fertilizer

SEE ALSO

- **MAKE HANGING BASKETS** >> 38/39
- **HERB HANGING BASKET** >> 206/207

SWEET TEMPTATIONS

Sweet fruits can tempt many garden pests, particularly slugs and birds, both of which find it more difficult to reach the fruits when plants are suspended in the air. This leaves ripe berries easy for you to harvest.

1 Place the basket in a pot to keep it stable while planting, and if it doesn't have an integral liner, line with durable plastic to retain soil and moisture. Cut drainage holes in the liner to prevent waterlogging.

Place the basket in a pot to keep it stable while planting

2 Water the plants in their pots. Add multi-purpose potting soil to the base of the basket, mixing in water-retaining crystals if desired, and arrange the plants so that the tops of the root balls are 1 in (2.5 cm) below the basket rim.

3 Fill around the plants with more soil, firming as you go. Make sure that the strawberries are not planted more deeply than they were in their original pots.

Ensure that the basket is not full to the rim, leaving space for watering

4 Soak the basket well and allow the water to drain before suspending it from a sturdy and well-secured bracket or hook. Water daily in warm weather and apply a liquid tomato fertilizer every two weeks once fruits appear.

PLANTING AN
APPLE TREE IN A POT

With their delicate spring blossoms and colorful crops, apple trees make beautiful features. Plant in large pots, place in a sunny site, and provide shelter from the wind to allow insects to pollinate the flowers.

YOU WILL NEED

- apple tree, e.g., a young dwarf variety
- large container pot
- broken plant pots
- soil-based potting mix
- slow-release fertilizer
- garden gloves

SEE ALSO

- **REPOTTING SHRUBS** >> 138/139
- **PLANT A TREE** >> 160/163
- **PRUNE AN APPLE TREE** >> 224/225

CARING FOR YOUR APPLE TREE

Once the apple tree is planted, never allow the soil to dry out, but avoid waterlogging. Cut out dead and diseased wood as soon as you see it. Repot every two years or as needed.

1 Add a layer of broken clay pots or gravel over the drainage holes to make sure that these do not become blocked and that water is allowed to flow away freely.

Choose a sturdy container suitable for housing the long, extensive roots of your apple tree

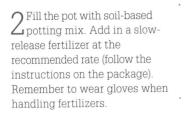

2 Fill the pot with soil-based potting mix. Add in a slow-release fertilizer at the recommended rate (follow the instructions on the package). Remember to wear gloves when handling fertilizers.

3 Water the tree, knock it from its pot, and check that the top of the root ball will sit 2 in (5 cm) below the new container's rim. Tease out the roots to help them establish.

4 Position the tree carefully in the center of the container. Fill around it with potting mix and firm, making sure that it is at the same level as it was in its original pot. Water well, and apply a mulch, leaving a space around the stem.

A miniature orchard is possible in a small garden with carefully grown and pruned fruit bushes and trees (such as these pear cordons), blackberries along a wall, and apples in a pot.

PRUNING AN
APPLE TREE

Annual pruning of apple trees will reward you with lots of blossoms, an abundance of fruit, and a beautifully shaped tree. Prune in winter when you can clearly see the branch structure.

YOU WILL NEED

- small pruning saw
- sharp pruning clippers
- garden gloves
- step ladder
- garden waste bag

SEE ALSO

- **REMOVE A BRANCH** >> 166/167
- **PRUNING KNOW-HOW** >> 236/237

AVOID
FALL PRUNING

Avoid pruning apple trees in fall because this may stimulate new growth that could suffer in winter. Winter is the best time to prune because the tree will be dormant.

1 Thin out young shoots as there is no room for them all to mature into fruiting branches. Leave about one or two young shoots to develop every 12in (30 cm). Also remove any short or weak growths.

2 Work around the tree systematically to create a balanced framework with an open center for good air circulation. Remove any upright branches or those growing at angles that distort the shape of the tree.

Make a clean cut to reduce the chance of disease entering the wound

3 Make your cut back to a main branch or to another of a similar size or smaller. Prune with restraint, as overpruned apple trees react vigorously the following year, making lots of leafy shoots with very few fruits.

SOFT FRUIT
IN **SMALL SPACES**

Fruit bushes and canes, including many berries and currants, are reliably productive and sparkle with colorful crops for much of the summer. A careful choice of varieties of fruit and larger pots means you can grow soft fruit in even the smallest garden

KEY POINTS

- **Birds enjoy** berries as much as we do. Before the berries start to ripen, put a fine net over the pot to keep them out.

- **Strawberries** are prone to disease and become less productive with age, so replace your plants every three years or so, using a clean pot and fresh potting soil.

- **SEE ALSO**

- **STRAWBERRY BASKET** >> 218/219
- **TREE FRUIT IN SMALL SPACES** >> 228/229

PRUNING SOFT FRUIT

For raspberries and blackberries, remove the old canes at the base after they have fruited. For fruit bushes, prune in winter, taking out dead and crossing wood to open out the center, and to keep the plant within bounds.

Closely related to the rampant, prickly hedgerow brambles, many modern types of blackberries are more compact, thornless, and have larger, sweeter fruits. Choose these forms for containers, and they will give you delicate white flowers then heavy crops of late-summer berries. Blackberries live for many years and are best planted in winter or spring in an 18in (45cm) pot of soil-based potting mix in full sun or partial shade.

Many berries, such as gooseberries, blackcurrants, and redcurrants can be expensive to buy at the store, but will grow well in containers of soil-based potting mix. They need a sunny spot with good air circulation to aid ripening. Do not allow the soil to dry out and water plants regularly, but not heavily, in dry weather to prevent the fruits splitting. Redcurrants and blackcurrants need a pot at least 18in (45cm) wide and deep. Gooseberries will grow in 15in (38cm) pots.

Gooseberries come in green, red, and yellow varieties

Grow different types of strawberries to ensure your pot, or strawberry planter, as here, produces berries over a long period of time. There are early-, mid-, and late-season varieties. Provide good drainage and feed plants fortnightly with tomato fertilizer once the berries have formed.

Blueberries are well suited to pots as they thrive in acid soil, which may not be the type in your garden. Plant in ericaceous potting soil in a 15in (38cm) pot in full sun or part shade. Net them against birds once the fruit develops. Here, a cane wigwam with garden netting is used.

TREE FRUIT IN
SMALL SPACES

Fruit trees can be trained to grow as cordons (single-trunked trees) ideal for packing lots of tasty fruit into small spaces. Mix varieties when choosing apples and pears, to ensure good pollination and crops.

KEY POINTS

- **Apple and pear** varieties suitable for growing in this way bear their fruits on short side shoots (spurs) along the length of their stem, making them very productive for their size.

- **If you are growing** several varieties of apples or pears, you need to make sure that they are compatible with each other for pollination. Seek advice when you buy because not all varieties are capable of pollinating each other.

SEE ALSO

- **STRAWBERRY BASKET** >> 218/219

- **APPLE TREE POT** >> 220/221

- **SOFT FRUIT IN SMALL SPACES** >> 226/227

JARGON BUSTER

Cordons are single-trunked trees on dwarfing rootstocks, which means that their size is restricted. Apple and pear trees are most commonly grown as cordons.

Cordons Traditionally a cordon is grown at a 45-degree angle. Remove the first year's blossom from the trees after planting to encourage strong roots. Prune new growth to two buds each year at the end of summer to keep the tree compact.

Horizontal cordon Also known as a stepover, the horizontal cordon makes an interesting and productive edging to a path or border. Keep the side shoots short in summer to restrict its growth and channel its energy into producing fruit.

Provide sturdy support, especially for a young tree

Columnar apples A columnar tree is bred to grow in a vertical, columnar shape with its fruit borne on compact spurs close to the main stem. It needs little summer pruning. Four dessert cultivars are available: 'Bolero,' 'Polka,' 'Waltz,' and 'Flamenco.'

Crop choices Many apple and pear varieties are available to grow as cordons or as compact bushes. You can buy them pretrained to give immediate structure in your garden. Choose mature specimens that are ready to fruit if you want instant impact.

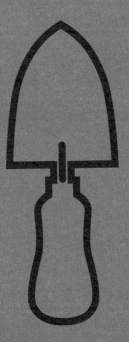

PRACTICALITIES

WATERING
PLANTS

During the heat of summer, it helps to be organized when watering so you can target only the areas in the garden that need attention, and avoid wasting water on those areas that do not.

KEY POINTS

- **If you water for long enough** in one place, moisture penetrates deep into the soil and plant roots grow down in search of it.
- **If you water lightly** and dampen only a top layer of soil, the roots will come up to the surface where they are vulnerable to drought.
- **Avoid overfilling containers** with potting mix, but leave a gap to allow water to pool and sink in.

SEE ALSO

- **KNOW YOUR SOIL** >> 12/13
- **LAWN CARE** >> 70/73

SAVING WATER

Rainwater can be collected in barrels positioned at down spouts. "Gray" water (from baths, showers, and basins) can be recycled, provided that it is not polluted with detergents or other cleaning agents.

What to water You should only need to water newly planted specimens, container plants, and freshly laid sod. Planting plants that live for two years or more between mid-fall and mid-spring reduces the amount of watering needed during the critical period when roots are establishing; unless there's a drought, these new additions won't need much summer watering.

Create a water reservoir around
a new plant by making a shallow
depression with a raised edge

Watering efficiently Water in the early morning or evening; if you water in the heat of the day moisture evaporates rapidly. Target the roots directly with a gentle flow or trickle and allow water time to soak in—avoid blasting the ground with a strong jet as this will erode the soil and expose roots. Don't use sprinklers—if you water foliage from above, much of it evaporates or is deflected.

Seep hose Sometimes called a leaky hose or trickle irrigation, this consists of a pipe perforated with numerous small holes. This pipe is attached to an outside faucet with leak-proof connectors, and laid directly on the soil surface, weaving between plants and, if necessary, is held in place with wire clips.

Watering containers As pots are watered frequently, the potting mix quickly erodes to expose roots, especially in the case of shallow-rooting species, like box. Try watering onto a piece of clay pot, to help dissipate the flow, or use a mulch of bark or some gravel, to avoid moisture loss.

Hoses and sprayer attachments Watering with a hose is less wasteful when you attach a sprayer with an on-off finger trigger. Sprayers have a broad head and the flow rate can be adjusted from a strong jet to a gentle shower, the latter setting being much less likely to cause soil erosion.

MAKING YOUR OWN **COMPOST**

Make the most of a quiet corner of your garden with a compost bin, and turn kitchen peelings and garden waste into valuable compost for free. There are bins to fit plots of every size, and the rich compost they generate can be used to give your plants a nutrient boost year after year.

KEY POINTS

- **Find a suitable site** for a compost heap or bin in full sun or part shade. Also place the bin on soil rather than a paved surface to provide access for creatures that help the composting process.

- **Add water to a heap** if it looks too dry. Remember, the composting process needs both moisture and air to circulate.

SEE ALSO

- **IMPROVE YOUR SOIL** >> 16/17
- **CHOOSING POTTING SOIL** >> 18/19

BIN ESSENTIALS

A compost bin must have an open base, a lid, and space to turn the heap. Also try to match the size of the bin to the amount of organic waste that your garden or kitchen will generate.

Filling your bin Try to achieve an equal balance of nitrogen-rich green material, such as spent vegetable plants and kitchen peelings, and drier carbon-rich waste, like dead leaves, small twigs, and shredded paper. Do not compost cooked foods, which attract vermin. Mix different types of waste, rather than creating thick layers, to allow moisture and air to circulate.

Turning the compost Waste breaks down faster in the warm, damp center of a compost heap than at the cool, dry edges, so for all the material to break down evenly it needs to be "turned." Wait until the bin is full and then turn the contents onto the soil, mix them together, and then put them back again. Don't add more waste; the compost should be ready to use in a few months.

OTHER FORMS OF COMPOST

Making leaf mold
Fallen fall leaves are a valuable resource because they break down to form dark, crumbly leaf mold, which is an excellent soil improver. Leaf mold is easy to make, by gathering up damp leaves and placing them in a plastic sack. Tie the top, pierce with a garden fork, and place it somewhere shady for two years while the leaves decompose.

Leaf mold is an excellent soil improver for raised beds and containers

Using worm farms Worm farms are good for small gardens where there is less waste to compost. Specially designed plastic containers, with good drainage and ventilation, house composting worms to break down organic matter into a fertile soil improver. Feed them with leafy garden waste.

Bokashi composting Wheat bran inoculated with microorganisms is used to ferment organic material, including vegetable scraps, meat, fish, and dairy products. The process does not produce odors, and a sealed container keeps away flies, making bokashi ideal for indoor composting.

HOW AND WHEN
TO PRUNE

Pruning keeps plants healthy, can restrict their size, and enables them to produce their best display of flowers, fruits, stems, or foliage. Most pruning tasks can be carried out annually, but those outlined here are best tackled as soon as problems are seen.

KEY POINTS

- **Buds and young shoots** can be damaged by spring frosts. Prune plants back to healthy, unfrosted buds to prevent dieback or diseases from starting at the frosted points.

- **Reversion is when leaves** of a variegated plant turn pure green. When you see any shoots showing signs of reversion, remove them completely using pruners.

SEE ALSO

- **REMOVE A BRANCH** >> 166/167
- **PRUNE AN APPLE TREE** >> 224/225

DEADHEADING TO PROMOTE FLOWERING

The removal of dead flower heads encourages some flowering plants to produce more blooms. Most faded flowers can be snapped off with the fingers.

Dead wood on a hornbeam

Coral spot on a branch

Cutting out dead and diseased wood Whenever you see dead or diseased wood on any tree or shrub, remove it immediately. If dead wood is left on a plant, disease can enter more easily and it may move down the stems, attacking healthy growth. Dead wood also looks unsightly. When a tree or shrub has been damaged, its natural defenses will eventually make a barrier in the form of a slight swelling between the live and dead wood. In this instance, remove the dead wood above the barrier.

Dealing with twin leaders

Twin leaders occur at the top of a tree when two stems of similar vigor grow close together. Remove the weaker stem using pruners. If left unpruned, the stems will try to grow away from each other, causing a weakness to develop. One stem may then break away from the tree, causing serious damage. Although this may not happen until the tree is much older, prompt action when the plant is young will prevent future problems.

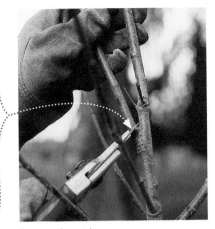

Remove the weaker stem

A single leader has strength

A water sprout growing from below the graft (knobbly bulge) on a rose

Removing water sprouts A water sprout is a vigorous, strong growth that emerges from a point low on a plant, close to the root system. If left, it can choke the plant or reduce its vigor. Such shoots are normally found on plants that have been grafted, such as roses, and usually look different from the rest of the plant. If seen early on, remove such a shoot by quickly tugging it away with a gloved hand or, if it has grown too large, remove the shoot using pruners.

CARING FOR
YOUR TOOLS

Using the right pruning tools and correct safety equipment helps to ensure that pruning is safe and enjoyable, and that you do not spread infections from plant to plant. You will also protect yourself against accidents if your equipment is well maintained, and extend the life of your tools.

CLEANING PRUNERS

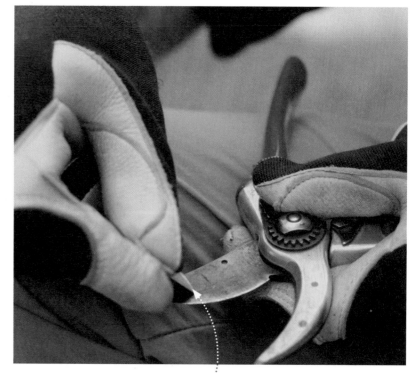

1 When pruning, plant sap dries and sticks to the blades, making them stiff. Scrape off the sap using a piece of metal with a straight edge, such as a metal plant label or penknife.

YOU WILL NEED

- piece of metal with a straight edge, such as a penknife
- steel or wire wool
- coarse brush
- lubricating oil
- cleaning cloth
- garden gloves

SEE ALSO

- **PRUNING KNOW-HOW** >> 236/237
- **PREVENT DISEASE** >> 246/247

SAFETY TIPS

Wear gloves when using sharp tools, and protective goggles when using electric trimmers; also, for the latter, use an emergency circuit breaker.

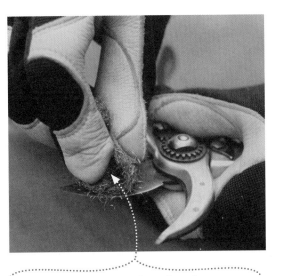

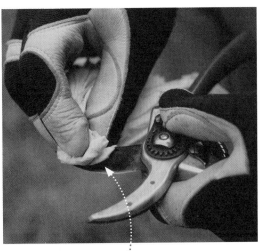

2 Then rub the blade with steel wool to remove any remaining dried sap and rust or other material. To prevent accidental cuts, wear gloves while cleaning your blades.

3 When the blade is clean, rub on some lubricating oil. This guards against rusting, and keeps the pruners sharp and clean while they are being stored.

CLEANING PRUNING SAWS

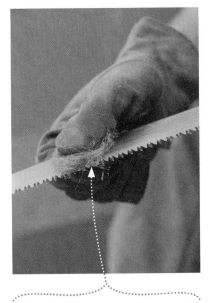

1 When you have finished pruning, use a coarse brush to remove any sawdust lodged in the saw's teeth. If this is left it can harden and reduce the saw's cutting ability.

2 Next, use steel wool to rub both sides of the saw blade. This removes dried sap and dirt, which can also make the saw less efficient.

3 Before putting the saw away after cleaning, rub some lubricating oil onto it with a cloth to protect the blade from rusting.

Bees are efficient pollinators and help make your garden grow. Choose plants that will bloom from early spring to early fall to attract these welcome visitors for as many months as possible.

TROUBLESHOOTING **WEEDS**

Weeds are an unfortunate fact of life in the garden, but by weeding from the start of the first growing season, you will gradually reduce the number that appear year after year. More persistent weeds may need special treatment: here's a guide to the worst offenders and how to manage them.

KEY POINTS

- **Why weed?** It is often said that a weed is nothing more than a plant in the wrong place. This is true, but many common weeds will quickly overrun a garden.

- **Clearing a lawn** of weeds can be done simply enough with a fork, a kitchen knife, or a hand weeder.

- **A garden hoe** is useful for removing young weed seedlings from beds.

SEE ALSO

- **LAWN CARE** >> 70/73

- **DEAL WITH PESTS** >> 244/245

- **PREVENT DISEASE** >> 246/247

FRIEND OR FOE?

Dandelions are a valuable source of food for many pollinators. If you can bear it, spare a patch of your garden to let dandelions flower for bees and hoverflies. You can deadhead them after flowering to stop them from seeding.

Bindweed This twining climber scrambles over plants and chokes them. Wiry stems, heart-shaped leaves, and white or pink trumpet-shaped flowers are produced by a network of white roots. The smallest piece of root produces a shoot. Dig out roots or, if the weed is very persistent, treat the shoots by painting on a herbicide.

Dock leaves
are useful,
however, to
treat stings
if nettle is
nearby

Stinging nettle The stinging hairs on the foliage can make brushes with this weed painful. Small plants often lurk undetected in borders. Long-lived nettles spread quickly just under the soil by thin runners, which soon form new plants. Dig out the plant (wearing gloves), ensuring that all runners and young plants are removed.

Dock With its soft, lush foliage, dock is a large weed often found in beds and borders, and sometimes in grass. It grows from a long, deep tap root that snaps off easily and must be removed from the soil to prevent the plant from regrowing. Keep removing the top growth to kill single plants.

Japanese knotweed A pernicious weed with fast-growing, rather attractive stems up to 6ft (2m) tall, clothed densely with lush, heart-shaped leaves. It has a tough, rampaging rootstock and the tiniest piece of root can form a new colony. Repeated applications of herbicide and removal of plants may eventually prove effective.

Common ragwort Usually found in lawns, this short-lived weed has hairy, rather unpleasant-smelling leaves with ruffled margins. Yellow daisylike flowers appear on tall stems and are cut by mowing. It is unsightly and poisonous to livestock. Pull out the rosettes by hand or with a hand weeder before the plant sets seed.

DEALING WITH
PESTS

Healthy plants can withstand pests more readily than those that are struggling. However, pests can still damage healthy plants, causing loss of crops or flowers, or even death. Use nonchemical methods first, and pesticides only as a last resort.

KEY POINTS

- **Welcome friendly predators** that eat pests. A few logs in a corner will shelter ground beetles and other beneficial insects.

- **Avoid growing similar plants** in the same spot for too long, especially soft fruits and vegetables, as they may become more likely to succumb to pests over time.

SEE ALSO

- **WEEDING OUT** >> 242/243
- **PREVENT DISEASE** >> 246/247
- **GARDEN FRIENDS** >> 248/249

BOTTLE BARRIERS

Protect vulnerable young plants using physical barriers made from plastic bottles (above). Cut the bottoms off clear plastic drink bottles and place them over the plants to help protect them from slugs and snails.

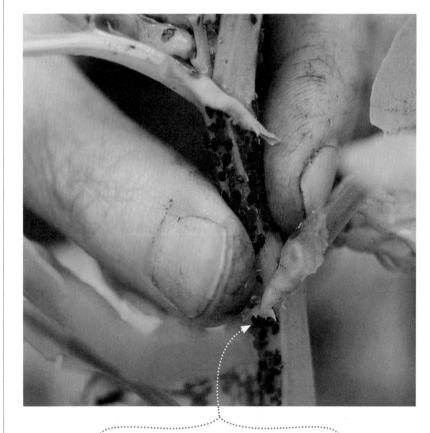

Act quickly As soon as you spot a pest, remove it, even if there is no damage to be seen. Clean aphids from shoots by squeezing them between your fingers; pluck slugs and snails from foliage and dispose of them.

Resort to chemicals Sometimes, severe pest attacks may threaten to kill a plant. In these cases, responsible use of pesticides will deal swiftly with the problem, causing minimal damage to beneficial creatures.

Ants When ants build their nests in the lawn or in planted containers, they may affect plant growth and become a nuisance. However, unless particularly troublesome, they are best left alone.

Aphids Also called greenfly or blackfly, these sap-suckers affect many plants, especially roses, distorting growth and spreading disease. Encourage ladybugs as predators.

Slugs and snails The best known of garden pests, these voracious feeders eat soft plant material, usually at night, decimating plants such as hostas.

Remove weeds and garden waste that may be home to slugs and snails

PREVENTING
DISEASES

When plants look unwell and there is no sign of any pests, a plant disease may be the cause. There are ways to minimize the risk of disease, and if you can identify common problems, you should be able to treat plants quickly.

KEY POINTS

- **Keeping plants healthy** can reduce the risk of disease: outbreaks of disease are often worse when plants are under stress due to lack of water or nutrients.
- **When buying a new plant,** check that it is healthy and suited to its intended position. This, along with good aftercare, helps prevent problems later.

SEE ALSO

- **CHOOSE HEALTHY PLANTS** >> 20/21
- **WEEDING OUT** >> 242/243
- **DEAL WITH PESTS** >> 244/245

PLANT VIRUSES

Viruses usually cause distorted foliage growth or strange color breaks in flowers. The virus particles are present in the sap of infected plants and can be spread by aphids. Affected plants are usually destroyed.

Removing contaminants An important part of looking after healthy plants is to keep the garden tidy. This includes removing and disposing of diseased plant material, such as fallen rose leaves infected with black spot. Old, fallen foliage can cause further infection, as spores released from the fungus on the leaf are spread around in the air.

Prevention and cure While keeping plants in good health and removing materials that may harbor disease can help prevent outbreaks, sometimes the only option is to use a chemical, such as a fungicide, to cure infected plants. A combination of prevention and cure is usually the best way to deal with plant diseases.

If spraying fungicides, always follow the instructions and use protective gear as recommended

COMMON DISEASES

Black spot This fungal disease, spread by splashing rain or in the air, causes black spots, sometimes with yellow margins, on leaves. Chemical controls are effective, and good plant care and hygiene are important.

Powdery mildew This silvery-white fungus affects the leaves of many plants, which eventually yellow and then fall. Dry conditions are often to blame, so keep plants moist and spray with a suitable fungicide if necessary.

Rust A fungal disease, this produces orange patches on the undersides of leaves, causing them to fall early. Remove infected material, improve air circulation, and spray with a suitable fungicide.

KNOW YOUR
GARDEN FRIENDS

Some wild creatures help to pollinate plants, break down compost, and prey on pests, so make these friendly visitors welcome in your garden.

KEY POINTS

- **The best way to** encourage helpful wildlife into the garden is to provide spaces for insects and birds to nest and to grow plants for them to feed, if possible, all year round.

- **Building homes for wildlife** can be as simple as leaving a small patch of the garden to grow wild, a pile of leaves unswept, or even making a small wildlife pond.

SEE ALSO

- **WEEDING OUT** >> 242/243

- **DEAL WITH PESTS** >> 244/245

- **PREVENT DISEASE** >> 246/247

BEE HOUSE

Solitary bees are excellent pollinators, but they can struggle to find nesting sites. A nesting box filled with drilled bamboo canes, or a log with drilled holes, will help encourage them into your garden.

Busy bees The flowers of many vegetables, such as runner beans, need to be pollinated by insects in order to set their crop. Bees are excellent pollinators, so include ornamental flowers in your vegetable garden to entice them in.

Friendly pest predators

Not all insects found in the vegetable garden or flower bed are pests, and many of them prey on harmful insects that can destroy entire crops. It is well worth encouraging them into your plot to try and achieve a natural balance, where pest numbers are kept low. Most pesticide sprays, even organic ones, kill beneficial insects as well as pests, so are best used only as a last resort.

Hoverflies are essential allies
Sometimes mistaken for bees, the adults are great pollinators, while the larvae are voracious feeders on insect pests.

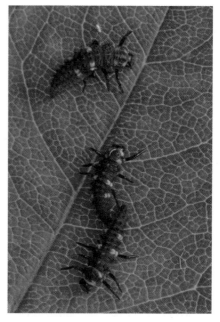

Ladybug larvae The adults are familiar (see opposite), but the less appealing larvae (above) enjoy feasting on juicy aphids.

Helpful animals and birds

Although they may be elusive, many larger garden residents, such as birds, can be extremely helpful in the garden, feeding on slugs and all kinds of other unwelcome visitors. Birds soon flock to gardens where food is provided and different species will pick off insects and even feed on snails while they are there. Create suitable habitats for all kinds of creatures and they will repay you with a healthier garden.

Brandling worms Smaller and redder than the usual earthworm, these creatures rapidly reduce vegetable matter to compost.

Frog Even a small pond can be home to many frogs and toads, which will help to keep slug numbers in check.

INDEX

ABOUT THE AUTHORS

The Royal Horticultural Society is the UK's leading gardening charity dedicated to advancing horticulture and promoting good gardening. Its charitable work includes providing expert advice and information, training the next generation of gardeners, creating hands-on opportunities for children to grow plants and conducting research into plants, pests, and environmental issues affecting gardeners.

For more information visit **www.rhs.org.uk** or call 020 3176 5800

This book is adapted from the following titles in the previously published **RHS Simple Steps** series:

Planting a Small Garden Phil Clayton

Plants for Shade Andrew Mikolajski

Family Garden Lia Leendertz

Easy-Care Garden Jenny Hendy

Containers for Patios Richard Rosenfeld

Climbing Plants Charles Chesshire

Lawns and Ground Cover Simon Akeroyd

Bamboos and Grasses Jon Ardle

Gardening Step by Step Phil Clayton, Jenny Hendy, Colin Crosbie, Jo Whittingham

Easy Pruning Colin Crosbie

Vegetables and Fruit in Pots Jo Whittingham

Vegetables in a Small Garden Jo Whittingham

Herbs William Denne

ACKNOWLEDGMENTS

The publisher would like to thank
Jo Hargreaves for proofreading and Christine Shuttleworth for the index.

Picture credits The publisher would like to thank the following for their kind permission to reproduce their photographs: (Key: a-above; b-below/bottom; c-center; f-far; l-left; r-right; t-top) 44 Dorling Kindersley: RHS Hampton Court Flower Show 2014 (tl). 65 Getty Images: Evan Sklar / The Image Bank (cr, br). 227 Dorling Kindersley: Alan Buckingham (tr); RHS Chelsea Flower Show 2011 (bl). 229 Garden World Images: Harry Smith Collection (bl).

All other images © Dorling Kindersley

For further information see: **www.dkimages.com**